NONFEASANCE

NONFEASANCE

"failure to act; *especially*: failure to do what ought to be done"

The Remarkable Failure of the Catholic Church to Protect Its Primary Source of Income

Michael W. Ryan

Church Revenue Protection

www.ChurchSecurity.info

Contents

Acknowledgements

While it is always risky to undertake the task of formally recognizing those individuals who contributed to the completion of a major undertaking such as this book, I would be remiss if I shrank from that task out of fear that I would miss someone. If I fail to mention any person who contributed to this effort, know that it was inadvertent and in no way a reflection of ingratitude on my part.

First and foremost, I thank my beloved spouse of the past 52 years, Shirley, who is the finest example of our Judeo-Christian heritage I have ever known. This project caused her much anguish, but she recognized and accepted my need to take it on and bring it to what we both hope and pray will ultimately prove to be a successful conclusion.

Next come my principal editors, Patricia and John, each of whom spent many hours pouring over the manuscript and providing me with the highly insightful feedback I know has made this book a far better product than it otherwise would have been. If this work falls short of the mark in any way, it is through no fault or shortcoming of theirs.

Thanks also to sister Mary Ann as well as brothers James and Patrick for their valuable input. Along the way, I also received support from sister Jane and brother John, too.

Special thanks to Rev. James A. Coriden and Rev. Thomas P. Doyle for their expert opinions in regard to Canon Law. Special thanks also go to my nephew, Tim, who provided valuable, firsthand information on Sunday collection procedures in one particular diocese, and to Peter whose epiphany provided a striking example of innocence lost as a direct result of the hierarchy's nonfeasance.

Finally, my sincere thanks go out to the many friends and relatives who, upon learning of my mission, offered their encouragement and advice, including personal thoughts and recollections of occurrences and procedures observed within their respective parishes.

To all of the above I extend my heartfelt thanks for your assistance and unflagging support.

Preface

As a Catholic boy growing up in the 1940s, I attended Saint Peter School in Skokie, Illinois and, following in my older brothers' footsteps, became an altar boy. In those years, being an altar boy was an honor that was conferred in about the fifth grade. In addition to learning the physical aspects of serving on the altar (when and where to stand, sit and kneel, etc.), the nuns taught us the Latin prayers and responses we had to recite at various points in the liturgy. As I recall, the lengthiest of those prayers was the *Confiteor* ("I confess") that, in essence, is an admission of sinfulness and a plea for the intercession of the saints with God on behalf of the individual.

Truth be told, this fifth grader understood only a fraction of what he was reciting. Nevertheless, and although I had no awareness of it at the time, my years as an altar boy helped create an unbreakable bond between myself and the Catholic faith, a bond that remains intact to this day.

Upon graduating from the eighth grade in 1950, I once again followed in my brothers' footsteps and became a soda fountain clerk at a local drugstore. I held that job through most of my high school years, and it was there that I first learned how to handle money. Mechanical (as opposed to electric) cash registers were the standard in those years, and I became adept at making change and ensuring that the cash register did not come up short at the end of my shift.

When I graduated from high school, I was not initially drawn toward college. I had worked a few summer jobs during high school and continued in the last such job following graduation. It was general warehouse work, however, and I left it for an opportunity to enter the then Post Office Department (POD). Once again, I found myself handling money, this time as a window clerk. In addition, I learned how the POD combined security devices and procedures to protect cash and other high-value items from theft, particularly theft by employees. While I didn't dwell on it at the time, it was apparent those systems not only prevented thefts but also tended to suppress - if not eliminate - the temptation to steal.

At the same time I was enjoying my newfound career, I also began to recognize the value of a college education. After less than one year with the post office, I applied and was accepted at Loyola of Chicago. I completed my degree over the course of five years while working at the post office part-time during the school year and full-time during the summers. By the time I graduated, I was married and had developed an attachment to the POD. Consequently, I resumed working full-time. In those five years, I had also become aware of the Postal Inspection Service - the law enforcement, audit and security arm of the POD - and I set my sights on entering that service.

On July 24, 1963, I was sworn in as a United States Postal Inspector. My duties included the investigation of various postal crimes within my assigned geographic area. I also conducted numerous financial audits. In the case of smaller post offices, I performed the audits by myself and, on rare occasions, determined that a postmaster or clerk had converted postal funds to his or her own use. Those occasions were rare because the POD had in place very stringent guidelines and procedures that had the effect of discouraging would-be embezzlers.

Embezzlements had to be reported to the U.S. Attorney of the district in which they occurred as well as to postal management. Almost invariably, the individual was fired regardless of whether or not the U.S. Attorney chose to prosecute them. After more than five years in the field, I had an opportunity to enter the management side of the Postal Inspection Service and I did so. Between 1969 and the year of my retirement, I worked at all levels of the Inspection Service and gained a broad range of experience in various operations including those relating to revenue protection.

My purpose in outlining my personal history to the extent that I have is not to impress the reader. Indeed, my work history pales in comparison to many others. Rather, the point I wish to make is that, at the time of my retirement, I had accumulated a substantial amount of hands-on experience regarding the workings of cash operations, and the safeguards that must be present in order to protect those operations from attack by employees as well as by outsiders.

The title of this book, NONFEASANCE, was chosen, in part, for its connection to the Catholic Church's present version of the *Confiteor*. That version emerged from the Second Vatican Council and was incorporated into the liturgy circa 1970. The prior version, the one I had memorized and recited as an altar boy, was longer but did not include any reference to "what I have failed to do." It would appear a majority of the prelates and theologians who participated in Vatican II grasped the importance of acknowledging the concept and existence of sins of omission. In doing so, they implicitly recognized the concept of nonfeasance and the fact that it can be sinful. The definition of nonfeasance that appears below the title of this book was taken from Version 2.5 of the Merriam-Webster Collegiate Dictionary.

The intent of this book is to accomplish what more than twenty years of communication have (at this writing) failed to accomplish, and that is to cause a fundamental reform in the way the Catholic Church handles its principal source of income: the Sunday collection. Historically and to the present day, the amount and type of protection afforded the Sunday collection has largely been the sole purview of each pastor, augmented by any specific guidance the local bishop might choose to offer. As the Catholic Church in America is comprised of nearly 18,000 parishes spread between 195 dioceses and archdioceses, one can easily understand how that protection would and, in fact, does vary between virtually nonexistent and acceptable.

One can also understand how wise, logical and desirable it would be for the hierarchy to formulate and implement standardized procedures that ensure the presence of an effective level of protection for Sunday collections Church-wide. And that brings us to the root of the problem: the U.S. Conference of Catholic Bishops (USCCB), formerly the National Conference of Catholic Bishops/U.S. Catholic Conference (NCCB/USCC), which has rejected all calls for the development and conference-wide implementation of genuinely secure Sunday collection procedures.

Given the purpose of this book, portions of it necessarily reference clergy and laypersons who have embezzled or misappropriated church funds. In light of that, I take this opportunity to acknowledge and thank the thousands of clergy and lay persons who, day after day, give willingly and unselfishly of their time and talent to bring Christ's message of love and service to all. It is for these honest, selfless, unsung heroes, and for the faithful in general, that I have written this book.

Finally, because I view the Catholic hierarchy as bearing ultimate responsibility for the vast majority of all Sunday collection embezzlements that have occurred over at least the past thirty-five years, I have withheld from the case histories cited in this book the names of all laypersons as well as any clergy below the level of bishop. Readers who would like to know more about a particular case are free to research the available footnotes.

I take no joy in recounting this saga of benign neglect.

Chapter I

Perception and Reality

*He said this not because he cared about the poor
but because he was a thief and held the money bag
and used to steal the contributions.* John 12:6

A well-known and widely accepted axiom holds that people and things are not always what they appear to be. Take, for example, that five, ten or twenty-dollar bill many churchgoers place in the collection basket each Sunday. They do so in the belief that their church has in place procedures that ensure that every dollar placed in the collection basket is properly deposited into the parish bank account. Perhaps you're one of those who donate by check or electronic transfer. If so, you might already be saying to yourself, "This book doesn't concern me; my donations are safe." That would be a mistake, however, because any loss of revenue, regardless of what form it takes, adversely impacts the parish as a whole. All donors rightfully assume their gifts are protected from theft but, more often than not, the reality is that the opposite is true: their gifts are highly vulnerable to theft.

Headquartered in Austin, Texas, the Association of Certified Fraud Examiners (ACFE) issues a biannual report that, among other objectives, "categorizes the ways in which serious fraud occurs and measures the losses organizations suffer as a result of occupational fraud."[1] The ACFE defines "occupational fraud" as: "The use of one's occupation for personal enrichment through the deliberate misuse or misapplication of the employing organization's resources or assets."[2] In a report entitled, "2008 Report to the Nation on Occupational Fraud & Abuse," the ACFE revealed the results of their analysis of nearly 1000 cases of occupational fraud investigated by Certified Fraud Examiners (CFEs) between January of 2006 and February of 2008. Some of their findings have relevance for churches and other non-profits.

Of particular note is the ACFE's declaration that "lack of adequate internal controls was most commonly cited as the factor that allowed fraud to occur."[3] The report also noted that:

the implementation of anti-fraud controls appears to have a measurable impact on an organization's exposure to fraud;

the typical U.S. organization loses 7% of its annual revenues to fraudulent activity;

occupational fraudsters are generally first-time offenders;

the majority of asset misappropriation schemes focus on cash, as opposed to other organizational assets; and

approximately 85% of all asset misappropriation cases in our study involved the theft or misuse of cash.[4]

The ACFE's findings, coupled with the fact that a very substantial portion of the Catholic Church's revenue comes to it in the form of cash donations received in the weekly collections, should provide all of the rationale anyone could possibly need to justify the adoption and Church-wide implementation of genuinely secure procedures ("anti-fraud controls") for receiving, storing, counting and banking Sunday collection funds.

The central issue is not the amount of money the Church is losing due to the absence of adequate internal controls. Rather, it is the fact that the hierarchy, as represented by the USCCB, has repeatedly rejected all calls to develop and implement such controls, well knowing the absence of those controls has fostered - and continues to foster – repetitive thefts from the Sunday collections as well as the moral lapses those thefts represent *and* facilitate.

If you could follow your Sunday offering in a typical church, this is pretty much what you would observe:

At the end of their collection route, all of the ushers meet at the rear of the church where the collection baskets are emptied into a larger basket or other unsecured container such as a canvas sack. One of the ushers then takes custody of that unsecured container and transports it to the altar, sacristy or rectory. In the Catholic Church, it is often brought to the altar at the Offertory when other members of the congregation bring the wine and communion hosts to the altar.

If the container is taken to the altar, it might be left there or handed to a server who then takes it to the sacristy. If it is taken to the sacristy, it remains there – in the open or in a cabinet or safe to which others have access - until it is taken to the rectory. That might be a half-hour or more after the service has ended and several persons have had lone, unobserved access to the container. If it is taken directly to the rectory, the usher might hand it over to whomever answers the door, or he might take it to the designated counting room that might or might not be staffed at the time.

In those parishes where a Saturday evening Mass or service is held, the collection gets the same treatment, but probably spends an additional 12–18 hours unsecured in a drawer, cabinet or safe that, even if locked, is nevertheless accessible to various people including clergy, staff and others having legitimate access to the rectory. When it is time to begin the count on Sunday or Monday (as is the case in some parishes), someone retrieves the unsecured containers and brings them to the counting area.

During the counting process, which might begin with only one or two counters present, people often move about and socialize to relieve the tedium connected with this task. At some point, someone makes a final tally and prepares the bank deposit. Often, that facet of the operation is not verified, being handled by one particular person who then puts the funds into a bank deposit bag. The bag, which might or might not be sealed, is then either taken to the bank (perhaps the night depository) or is placed in a drawer, cabinet or safe for overnight retention pending deposit the next day. In some parishes, the collection is counted on Sunday but is not secured in a bank deposit bag until Monday when someone else verifies the count, makes up the deposit slip and transports it to the bank.

So what's wrong with the above-described processes? In a nutshell, the collection funds are not brought under *positive* control until they appear on a bank deposit slip several handlings and as much as 40 hours following the first Mass or service. No business of any size would survive more than a few months if it failed to establish *positive control* over its revenue at the point of receipt. In a church's case, that point (practically speaking) is when the ushers first meet to consolidate their collection baskets into a single container.

Before any Sunday collection system can be deemed adequately secure, appropriate security equipment and procedures must be applied so that no one - not even the pastor - has lone, unobserved access to those funds or any portion thereof. Once established, that mantle of protection must remain absolutely unbroken until all monies have been accurately tallied, recorded and properly deposited into the church bank account. Until the final steps (recording and deposit) are reached, the cash portion of each week's collections is quite literally there for the taking; it's anybody's money.

Strictly speaking, a church is not a business, at least not in the commercial *profit and loss* sense. But all churches depend upon the receipt of a steady stream of income sufficient to cover their overhead (salaries, maintenance, utilities, etc.) and provide the services they are committed to providing their parishioners as well as other members of the community in which they reside. Any unlawful or inappropriate drain on that income stream negatively impacts the church's ability to fulfill its mission of service to its members as well as to the community at large.

It is impossible to predict who will or will not be tempted by easy access to unsecured collection funds. It could be an usher, a counter, an altar server, a rectory employee, a teacher, a pastor or associate pastor, a music or choir director or anyone else having lone, unobserved access to the collection or any portion thereof. Further, such access includes both assigned access and what can be called "constructive" access. Ushers and counters, for example, have assigned access; their duties require direct contact with the collections. A church secretary whose duties do not include involvement in the collection, counting or deposit of funds would, in all likelihood, have constructive access by virtue of the fact that she has access to the safe or security cabinet in which the collections are stored pending the counting and banking process.

Much has been written about violations of trust committed by persons previously thought to be paragons of virtue. Consider the case of St. Mary Magdalen Church in Oakville, Connecticut, that had been unable to pay its bills for several years. Finally, in January of 1983, the parish priests asked local authorities to investigate what they suspected was skimming from the Sunday collections. As a result of the investigation that followed, a parishioner who was once dubbed "the saint of Oakville" was charged with embezzling $60,000 between Dec. 1, 1979, and Oct. 1, 1982. The parishioner was described in media coverage as being "Parish council president. Director of Confraternity of Christian Doctrine, or catechism. Vice president of the Catholic

Women's Club. Lector at the daily 8:45 a.m. Mass. Fundraiser. Counter and depositor of the Sunday collection."[5]

Although it occurred thirty years ago, the above-described case clearly illustrates the fact that persons reputed to be above reproach can succumb to the temptation presented by a vulnerable collection system. The task of securing a church's principal source of revenue cannot be achieved by anyone wearing rose-colored glasses. It must be approached with the worst-case scenario in mind, and without regard for personalities or preconceived notions about who can or cannot be trusted. Reliance upon trust is only appropriate <u>after</u> we've done everything possible to render its presence unnecessary. As Benjamin Franklin phrased it, "An ounce of prevention is worth a pound of cure."

The objective of this book is to accomplish what more than twenty years of correspondence have thus far failed to accomplish, and that is to cause a fundamental change in the way the Church's principal source of income (the Sunday collection) is handled. In an effort to achieve that objective, I must and will establish four particulars beyond reasonable doubt:

1.) that regardless of a church's size, there is essentially only one way to effectively secure a congregation's offerings between their placement into a collection basket and their deposit into the church's bank account;

2.) that to have a uniformly efficacious and lasting effect, genuinely secure procedures must be mandated from the highest level of church authority;

3.) that the hierarchy of the Roman Catholic Church in America, as represented by the U.S. Conference of Catholic Bishops (USCCB) has, for at least the past twenty years, intentionally shunned the Church-wide implementation of readily available, low-cost procedures that, properly implemented and monitored, would end virtually all currently ongoing Sunday collection embezzlements and prevent virtually all future such embezzlements; and

4.) that the failure of the USCCB to implement such procedures renders them ultimately responsible for virtually every loss of Sunday collection funds due to embezzlement as well as for the moral lapses of those who succumb (most often weekly) to the temptation presented by a highly vulnerable collection system.

Before I proceed to establish those four particulars, however, it might be helpful to gain some appreciation for the amount of money that most likely has been and is being lost to Sunday collection embezzlements. In that regard, the public's ability to appreciate and react to loss figures has been somewhat impaired by the ongoing national debate over the federal budget and deficit. It has gotten to the point where the mention of losses or savings amounting to a few billion dollars is deemed naive and unworthy of serious discussion or consideration. Readers should bear that tendency in mind while reading the next chapter. Congress' fiscal interplay aside, a billion dollars in church offerings can never be categorized as a trivial or negligible sum of money.

Chapter II

How Much Money Is the Church Losing?

Because, with few exceptions, the Church neither has nor ever has had any system or procedures in place to prevent or detect thefts from Sunday collections, no one can state with any degree of certitude how many embezzlements are ongoing at any given time *or* how much money is being lost as a result of those embezzlements. That bears repeating: *no one*, not the U.S. Conference of Catholic Bishops (USCCB), not the Diocesan Fiscal Management Conference (DFMC), not the National Leadership Roundtable on Church Management (NLRCM), and not any of the individuals, organizations, or institutions that have studied and reported on various aspects of the Catholic Church's fiscal operations, whether locally, nationally, or internationally. With virtually nothing in place to deter or detect embezzlements from the Sunday collections, it is impossible to *know* how much money has been or is being lost.

Sunday collection embezzlements can be likened to an iceberg. At the very top (for all to see) are those that are discovered, reported to the local bishop and aired in the local media. Next come those that are discovered and reported to the local bishop but are not aired in the local media. After all, no bishop seeks that kind of publicity; it's bad for morale, not to mention parishioners' enthusiasm for giving. Next come those embezzlements that are discovered but are not reported to the local bishop. Let's face it: few pastors are eager to expose themselves to the embarrassment that goes with admitting they were fooled by an employee or, worse, a member of their congregation. Finally, lying unseen at the bottom of the iceberg, are those embezzlements that are ongoing, having yet to be discovered. Undiscovered Sunday collection embezzlements can be likened to undiagnosed cancer; in all probability, the number of undiagnosed cases far exceeds the number of cases that have been diagnosed.

The USCCB and/or the DFMC might attempt to develop a loss estimate but, without secure procedures Church-wide, it could only be a guesstimate. They might also claim their parish audit programs (which vary from diocese to diocese due to the closely guarded autonomy of each local bishop) can and do identify Sunday collection embezzlements. Generally speaking, however, that would be a fallacy because you can't audit what was never recorded. Sunday collection embezzlements typically occur *before* the monies are counted and recorded; suspicion or telltale signs notwithstanding, there is no paper trail to audit.

Although total church embezzlements cannot be known exactly, there is value in estimating how much the Church has lost in years past and how much it is presently losing. By reasonably quantifying the impact inadequate Sunday collection security has had and most likely is having upon the Church's principal source of income, we can begin to understand why the Church-wide implementation of genuinely secure Sunday collection procedures is not merely a good idea or a reasonable request but, rather, an absolute imperative. I developed my estimate of losses by multiplying the estimated average annual loss per affected parish by the estimated number of affected parishes.

The first step in that process was to estimate the average annual loss resulting from an ongoing Sunday collection embezzlement. Data from reported case histories can inform this estimate, and full case-history information can help demonstrate the conservativeness of the estimate. Consider the case of the woman who pleaded "no contest" (rough translation: *If you say I'm guilty, I won't dispute it.*) to charges she embezzled $60,000 from the collections of St. Mary Magdalen parish in Oakville, Connecticut, between Dec. 1, 1979, and Oct. 1, 1982. According to that information, one might conclude she embezzled about $20,000 per year. The news report goes on to state, however, that when the parish priests began counting the collections themselves, "the receipts jumped from approximately $4,000 a month, as recorded by [name withheld], to $12,000 a month."[6]

This would be a good time to test our basic math skills. Assuming the collections increased from $4,000 to $12,000 per month, the increase comes to $8,000 per month or $96,000 per year, and the average weekly loss computes to more than $1,800! This case graphically illustrates the fact that prosecutors typically charge the embezzler with stealing an amount the prosecutor is satisfied can be easily proven in any court proceeding that might follow. Actual losses are often tens if not hundreds of thousands of dollars higher than what the individual is charged with stealing. If we were to use the prosecutor's figure in our database, we would assess that case as having caused losses averaging just over $400 per week when, as noted above, the true figure was most probably $1,400 per week higher.

A second example involves a man trusted to count the donations at Cathedral Santuario de Guadalupe in Dallas, Texas. He was sentenced to eight years in prison after he admitted stealing more than $240,000 from the collections. Given the job in 1986, his activities weren't discovered until 1991 when a church employee noticed discrepancies between amounts written on donation envelopes and daily totals. According to the Associated Press article, "after [name withheld] was told to stay home one day, collections jumped by $5,000, according to court records. [name withheld] confessed to [the pastor] in October 1991 and turned over $4,300 in cash. He later returned an additional $158,000 he had stashed and gave the church three cars and household furnishings he had bought with pilfered donations."[7] The AP article also noted the thefts occurred over a six-year period.

If collections suddenly increased by $5,000 per week as stated in the above article, we're looking at a quarter million dollars per year embezzlement. Using the amount he admitted stealing, however, the impression is given he was stealing between $40,000 and $50,000 per year, or somewhere in the neighborhood of $750 to $1,000 per week. In either case, there is no doubt he was exacting a heavy toll on that church's primary source of income.

One further point needs to be made, and that concerns pastor-directed deductions from the cash portion of the Sunday collections prior to their deposit into the parish bank account. At best, the practice is highly irregular and, in most cases, constitutes theft. Take, for example, the case of a former pastor of St. Anthony Church in North Providence, Rhode Island, who was indicted for embezzling (in various ways) $200,000 from his parish between 1985 and 1988. In regard to the Sunday collections, and according to a news article, the pastor "persuaded another parishioner who was a longtime friend to give him money from the weekly collections. Evidence shows the parishioner gave [name withheld] about $400 a week from weekly collections as far back as March 1985."[8] That constitutes theft, pure and simple, and the fact that the money was procured through an intermediary does nothing to mitigate the seriousness of the act or the pastor's culpability.

In light of the above examples, and recognizing it is virtually impossible to come up with a demonstrably accurate loss estimate, I opted to begin with what I believe to be a very conservative estimate of $25,000 per year (a little under $500 per week) for the average embezzlement in 2010. As for the estimated number of parishes whose Sunday collections I believe it is reasonable to assume are under attack at any given time, I chose a frequency of one in five, or twenty percent. Again, I believe that is a conservative estimate based upon the fact that, with few exceptions, the Church has virtually nothing in place to deter or detect such embezzlements. I'm confident most readers will conclude the loss projections developed using those two estimates are also conservative.

According to statistics developed by the Center for Applied Research in the Apostolate (CARA), a national, non-profit, Georgetown University affiliated research center, there were 17,958 Catholic parishes in America in 2010.[9] Twenty percent of that number totals 3,592 parishes, and multiplying that number by the estimated annual loss per affected parish ($25,000) results in a total estimated loss of $89.8 million for the Catholic Church in America in 2010 alone.

With a view toward putting that sum of money into context, consider the fact that during the four-year period ending December 31, 2010, Catholic Charities USA Disaster Operations supported 152 disaster recovery efforts nationwide, including the infamous BP Gulf Coast oil spill. Over the course of those four years, they awarded a total of 271 Disaster Relief Grants totaling $73 million to various local Catholic Charities agencies providing emergency services to more than one million people.[10] Assuming the 2010 Sunday collection loss projection is anywhere near being accurate, one can see that just one year's losses far exceed what Catholic Charities USA spent on disaster relief over the course of four years.

Another way to evaluate such a loss is to compare it with the universe to which it relates, in this case, the total amount given in the collections by American Catholics. While current figures are not available, a 2006 report by the USCCB included an estimate of Catholic giving to local parishes in the Sunday collections totaling $5.864 <u>billion</u> in 2002.[11] According to the 2002 edition of *The Official Catholic Directory*,[12] there were 19,496 U.S. Catholic parishes in 2002. Applying the Consumer Price Index to the $25,000 average loss estimate for 2010, the average loss due to Sunday collection embezzlements in 2002 are estimated at $20,456 per affected parish or

$79,758,000 overall. That represents 1.36 percent of the USCCB's estimate of Sunday collection revenue for that year.

Readers will recall from the previous chapter that, based upon a study of nearly 1000 cases of occupational fraud investigated by Certified Fraud Examiners (CFEs) between January of 2006 and February of 2008, the Association of Certified Fraud Examiners estimated the typical U.S. organization loses seven percent of its annual revenues to fraudulent activity.[13] According to the ACFE's 2002 report encompassing 663 cases of occupational fraud, six percent of total revenues were estimated to have been lost to occupational fraud in that year.[14]

While losses due to post-deposit embezzlements, that is, embezzlements committed after the collection funds have been properly deposited into the parish account, would also have to be taken into account for comparison against the 2002 ACFE estimate of six percent, it seems apparent from the figures outlined above that my estimate of losses due to Sunday collection embezzlements is conservative. Even if post-deposit losses totaled twice the amount I estimated for collection losses, the aggregate losses in 2002 would still be 32% below the ACFE's estimated six percent average.

My purpose here is not to convince the mathematicians, CPAs and economists that my figures are rock solid; that's simply not possible since we're discussing numbers that no one has any effective means of confirming. Rather, I am attempting to make the point that, given the number of parishes that in all probability are being victimized at any point in time, repetitive thefts from the U.S. Catholic Church's primary source of income can and do add up to very large sums of money. Using the 2010 per affected parish estimate of $25,000 as a base, and taking into account the fluctuating value of the dollar as determined by the Consumer Price Index (CPI), I developed a *real dollars* estimate of losses due to Sunday collection embezzlements for the forty-six-year period 1965 through 2010. The estimated losses for that period came to $2,317,036,000. That's $2.3 billion in round figures! A chart depicting the process used to calculate that figure is shown on the following page. If that amount of money, or any amount even remotely close to it, strikes you as being both plausible and worthy of your continued attention, you are invited – no, make that *urged* - to read on.

Estimate of Losses Due to Sunday Collection Embezzlements in the U.S. Catholic Church

Year	Annual Losses* (adj. for $ inflation)	Avg. Ann. Losses for periods shown	Total Losses for periods shown	Existing Parishes**	Avg. Annual Loss per Parish*
1965	$12,740,000			17,637	$3,612
1974	$19,707,000	1965-'74: $16,223,000	$162,230,000	18,427+++	$5,348
1975	$22,248,000			18,515	$6,008
1984	$44,961,000	1975-'84: $33,604,000	$336,040,000	19,171+++	$11,727
1985	$46,919,000			19,244	$12,190
1994	$65,220,000	1985-'94: $56,069,000	$560,690,000	19,322+++	$16,879
1995	$66,998,000			19,331	$17,330
2004	$80,799,000	1995-'04: $73,898,000	$738,980,000	18,935+++	$21,336
2005	$83,233,000	2005-10: $86,516,000	$519,096,000	18,891	$22,031
2010	$89,800,000			17,958	$25,000

Estimated Cumulative Losses 1965-2010: $2,317,036,000

* Annual loss figures are based upon an estimation that collections in 20% of existing parishes lost an average of $25,000 in CY 2010. Losses for other years shown were computed by applying the Consumer Price Index to the CY 2010 Average Annual Loss per Parish estimation.

** Center for Applied Research in the Apostolate, http://cara.georgetown.edu/CARAServices/requestedchurchstats.html.

*** Estimated from trend reflected by CARA figures for '65, '75, '85, '95, '05 and 2010 MMVR/4-15-11

Chapter III

It's Not Only About the Money

For the love of money is the root of all evils,
and some people in their desire for it
have strayed from the faith and have
pierced themselves with many pains.
1 Timothy 6:10

Note well, the phenomenon of Sunday collection embezzlement is not merely about the loss of money. It also concerns the impact of that act upon those who commit it, and the uses to which that money is subsequently put. Indeed, when viewed from the perspective of a believer's quest for eternal salvation, and those things that endanger one's ability to achieve that all-important goal, the loss of money is clearly the least important consideration.

Not infrequently, news reports of church embezzlements also contain information indicating the thief was using the money to pursue a vice of one sort or another, including gambling, pornography, and other sexual deviancies, the most heinous and destructive of which is the sexual abuse and exploitation of minors. An October 29, 2004, article by a *Seattle Post-Intelligencer* investigative reporter included this statement:

> In more than a dozen cases investigated by the Seattle Post-Intelligencer nationwide, priests accused of sexual abuse have also been accused of stealing from the church -- some were convicted and served jail time for stealing amounts upwards of $100,000. In other cases, the church either was not aware of the theft, or did not report it to the police, so the priests were not prosecuted.

> Many accusers have said the priests who abused them used money donated by parishioners to provide them with gifts and entertainment. They said they watched as their abusers counted the

collection every week without oversight -- and some said they repeatedly saw their pastor pocket cash donated by parishioners.[15]

Consider the case of a former San Francisco monsignor who was defrocked in 1994 after several men accused him of having molested them as boys. Two years later, the church paid a reported $2.5 million to settle sexual abuse claims brought by former young parishioners against the monsignor and other priests. After serving two years in jail on charges relating to the alleged molestation of nine former altar boys, the monsignor was freed when a judge ruled the statute of limitations had run out. In a relevant aside, the news article noted the monsignor was also charged with embezzling at least $250,000 in church donations.[16] While the article did not make the connection between the embezzlement and the altar boys' abuse, it does not take a great leap of imagination to connect them.

In another case, the former pastor of St. John the Baptist Church in Haverhill, Massachusetts, was charged with stealing $83,147 from his parish, more than $50,000 of which came from the collections. According to the newspaper article, the police investigation disclosed that much of the money was spent on a pornography habit. Evidence gathered by the police reportedly included cable TV bills establishing that pay per view "adult" movies totaling over $4,000 began the day the pastor came to the parish, and credit card records establishing the pastor purchased pornography over the Internet. The credit card reportedly had a balance of $25,000 on it when the investigation was conducted.[17]

In another case, the former business manager of St. Mary Catholic Church in Buffalo Grove, Illinois, was charged with stealing more than $600,000 in collections and other church funds over the course of five years to support a gambling habit that cost at least $1.8 million. While the newspaper article did not include an estimate of how much the business manager stole from the collections, it was reported that a typical Sunday collection at St. Mary's might total between twenty-five and thirty thousand dollars. Given those amounts, it's easy to see how several hundred dollars or more could be removed on any given weekend and not be missed. According to the article, after church officials began investigating the matter, they found opened offering envelopes in a wastebasket in the business manager's office.[18]

In a remarkably candid article, made so by the fact it was published in the Archdiocese of Milwaukee's own weekly newspaper, a staff writer highlighted a couple of then (2004) recent embezzlement cases and speculated about causative factors. The article,[19] entitled "Church embezzlement is theft, but also betrayal of trust," highlighted two cases in particular, both involving the Sunday collections. The first case involved a parish bookkeeper's embezzlement of more than $500,000 in collection funds from the Jesuit parish, Church of the Gesu, over the course of her eight-year employment. The second case involved a parish volunteer who, unbeknownst to the pastor of Saints Peter and Paul Parish, had a key to the vault in which the collections were stored each weekend pending the counting process; his forays into the collections were estimated to cost the parish more than $300,000.[20]

In each of those two cases, a substantial portion of the blame was attributed to the thieves' alleged addiction to gambling, a justification many would say is akin to invoking that old tongue-in-cheek excuse, "The devil made me do it." Indeed, the parish volunteer put it this way: "I convinced myself that God was actually helping me along. I said, 'God is providing for me.'"[21] One can only wonder whether he said that because he believed it or because he saw an opportunity to generate sympathy from those who would subsequently read the article. In either case, it's an economic and moral tragedy that could and should have been prevented.

Jesus left no doubt about his opinion of those who cause children to sin. In Mark 9:42, he declared, "Whoever causes one of these little ones who believe (in me) to sin, it would be better for him if a great millstone were put around his neck and he were thrown into the sea." I mention that because I had occasion to describe my book project to the husband of a relative. As I was explaining the theme of the book, he experienced an epiphany. He recalled that, as an altar boy in the mid-sixties, he had stuffed his pockets with cash from a collection basket that had been handed to him for transport to the sacristy during a Mass at which he was serving. Had the collection been secured in the manner that will be explained in the next chapter, that altar boy (now a devout Catholic and highly respected member of his community) would not have been tempted, let alone fallen into sin.

Finally, and lest we forget, there's good old-fashioned greed. Take, for example, the two pastors who took turns plundering St. Vincent Ferrer Catholic Church, in Delray Beach, Florida. The first pled guilty and was sentenced to fourteen months imprisonment in spite of the fact that he made restitution amounting to over $700,000. In levying the sentence, the judge called the crime "pure greed unmasked" and a "huge violation of trust."[22] The second priest, who succeeded the first as pastor of St. Vincent Ferrer, pled "not guilty" but was subsequently convicted and sentenced to four years in state prison. In imposing his sentence, the judge stated, "No matter how many good works you have performed in your many years as a priest, your legacy will always be one of thievery and deceit."[23]

In the next chapter, you will see that there is essentially only one way to ensure that every dollar placed into the collection baskets each weekend is, in fact, properly deposited into the parish bank account. As you read that chapter and those that follow, however, bear in mind the objective is not merely to protect the monetary assets of the Church, but to also protect the souls of those to whom those assets are exposed and entrusted.

Chapter IV

Why Only One Way to Secure a Collection?

In Chapter I, I stated I must establish four particulars beyond reasonable doubt:

1.) that regardless of a church's size, there is essentially only one way to effectively secure a congregation's offerings between their placement into a collection basket and their subsequent deposit into the church's bank account;

2.) that in order to have a uniformly efficacious and lasting effect, genuinely secure procedures must be mandated from the highest level of church authority;

3.) that the hierarchy of the Roman Catholic Church in America, as represented by the U.S. Conference of Catholic Bishops (USCCB) has, for at least the past twenty years, intentionally shunned the Church-wide implementation of readily available, low-cost procedures that, properly implemented and monitored, would end virtually all currently ongoing Sunday collection embezzlements and prevent virtually all future such embezzlements; and

4.) that the failure of the USCCB to implement such procedures renders them ultimately responsible for virtually every loss of Sunday collection funds due to embezzlement as well as for the moral lapses of those who succumb (most often weekly) to the temptation presented by a vulnerable collection system.

Taking those four particulars in order, we will begin with number one. Given the setting and atmosphere in which the average church receives its principal source of revenue - in a house of worship during a religious service - most readers will recognize that the use of cash registers or similar devices to accept and document each offering would be both unseemly and logistically impractical if not impossible. Yes, quite a few churchgoers give by check and some donate via credit or debit card authorizations, but a substantial segment of most congregations will always insist on giving cash.

Churchgoers could deposit their offerings into locked receptacles placed at strategic locations (entrances and exits) within the church but, in addition to giving rise to a whole new set of security issues, the liturgical symbolism of communal giving would be lost. The practice of passing the basket also serves as a stimulus to giving, and it is highly unlikely the Catholic Church will discard that ritual at any time in the foreseeable future. All things considered, the passing of the basket is the most practical means for a church to take custody of its members' donations when proffered during a religious service.

How the Experts View Accountability

The American Institute of Certified Public Accountants (AICPA), *the* professional association for Certified Public Accountants (CPAs) throughout the United States, has long recognized that the mere absence of mathematical discrepancies does not guarantee that all is well. In 1973 they issued an authoritative guideline entitled *Statement on Auditing Standards - Codification of Auditing Standards and Procedures,* several portions of which have particular application for churches and other cash-handling organizations. The first principle states, in pertinent part:

> Agreement of a cash count with the recorded balance does not provide evidence that all cash received has been properly recorded. This illustrates an unavoidable distinction between fiduciary and recorded accountability: the former arises immediately upon acquisition of an asset; the latter arises only when the initial record of the transaction is prepared.[24] (emphasis added)

In the case of a church's Sunday collection, fiduciary accountability begins when members of the congregation place their offerings into the collection basket. In a typical parish, however, the number of people (clergy, employees, and volunteers) having lone, unobserved access to the collection or a portion thereof prior to its tabulation and deposit (recorded accountability) would leave even the greenest of auditors aghast.

The second principle enunciated by the AICPA addresses that critical, often lengthy interval between the receipt and subsequent recording of assets, declaring:

> The objective of safeguarding assets requires that access be limited to authorized personnel. The number and caliber of

personnel to whom access is authorized should be influenced by the nature of the assets and the related susceptibility to loss through <u>errors</u> and <u>irregularities</u>. Limitation of direct access to assets <u>requires</u> appropriate physical segregation and protective equipment or devices.[25] (emphasis added)

The terms "errors" and "irregularities" are employed to differentiate between accidental and intentional wrongdoing, respectively. When one considers "the nature of the assets" involved in the Church's case – large amounts of currency - their "related susceptibility to loss" as a result of intentional wrongdoing should be glaringly evident. Note also the AICPA's use of the word "requires" as opposed to a less forceful word such as "suggests." In the context in which it is used, Merriam-Webster defines "require" as follows: "to demand as necessary or essential : have a compelling need for."[26]

Many churches have satisfactory, good or perhaps even excellent control over their disbursements and thus might conclude their revenue is secure. The third principle enunciated by the AICPA addresses that misconception as follows:

Controls and weaknesses affecting different classes of transactions are not offsetting in their effect. For example, weaknesses in cash receipts procedures are not mitigated by controls in cash disbursements procedures.[27]

For a church, of course, the "cash receipts procedures" encompass all stages of the Sunday collection process up to and including the deposit of all monies into the parish bank account. Having tight control over a church's disbursements while failing to implement secure cash receipts procedures can be likened to closing the pasture gate after the livestock has escaped; it might look good but, in reality, it's too little too late.

Finally, it is relevant to note that senior managers and key personnel have a tendency to cling to old policies and procedures in spite of the emergence of new technologies and more secure and efficient procedures. For those organizations whose continued existence depends upon their ability to show a financial profit, new technologies and more secure and efficient procedures are quickly adopted whenever they are seen as a way to improve the so-called "bottom line." But churches and other non-profit organizations lack the for-profit motive, and that absence can serve to strengthen, even institutionalize, that old, inane rationale which usually ends with the words "because this is the way we've always done it." The fourth principle enunciated by the AICPA is directed to those who are prone to take that position. That principle states:

> Management has the responsibility for adopting sound accounting policies, for maintaining an adequate and effective system of accounts, for safeguarding assets, and for devising a system of internal control that will, among other things, help assure the production of proper financial statements.[28]

From the four principles outlined above, it is apparent the accounting profession, as represented by its premier professional association, recognizes the need for special equipment and procedures when dealing with highly vulnerable assets such as cash donations. Let's now look at what is essentially the only practical way to apply those principles so as to effectively protect a church's Sunday collection.

The Collection Process

Upon completing their assigned collection routes, the ushers ordinarily meet at the rear of the church where they empty their baskets into a larger basket or sack that, more often than not, is then taken to the altar. Alternatively, it might be taken to the sacristy or rectory. In any case, and no matter what the next stop might be, the point at which the ushers meet to consolidate the contents of their collection baskets into a single container is the first practical opportunity to establish *positive control* over that service's collection, and it is absolutely essential that it be done at that point.

As used here, the term "positive control" refers to the act of securing the collection inside either a serially numbered, self-sealing, tamper-evident polyethylene bag, or a drawstring sack that is then closed and sealed with a tamper-proof numbered seal. Any delay in performing this critical step - which must be witnessed by two or more ushers - automatically exposes the collection to covert theft from that point forward. Two acceptable collection container alternatives are pictured on the next page.

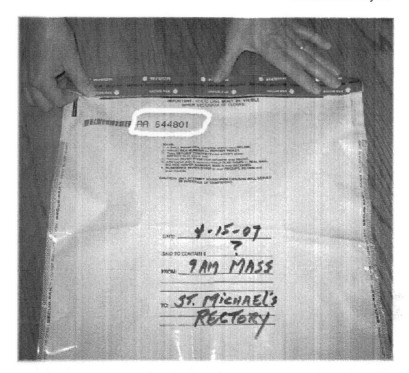

Serially-numbered, self-sealing, tamper-evident polyethylene bag

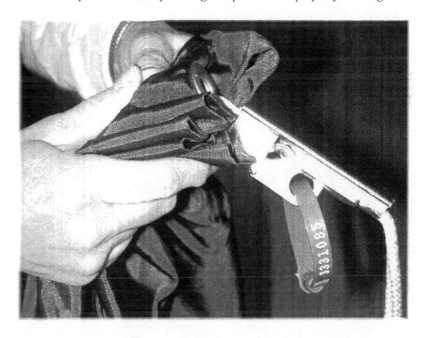

Drawstring Sack with Serially-numbered Tamper-proof Seal

It is essential that the serial numbers of the bags or seals assigned for use by the ushers each weekend be recorded by the designated bag/seal custodian. That person should have exclusive custody of the bulk supply of bags or seals, and cannot be someone who has access to the safe or other locked container in which the collections are stored pending the counting process. A separate record must be made of the serial numbers of the bags or seals received by the counters. Each week, those two records must be reconciled by someone who is not otherwise involved in the collection or counting process and, ideally, does not have access to the safe or other locked container where the collections are stored pending the counting process. Any discrepancy between the record of bags or seals assigned for use by the ushers, and the record of bags or seals received by the counters might well be indicative of theft and must be investigated.

The importance of this requirement was highlighted not long ago in the Archdiocese of Chicago that, in 2005, codified and disseminated the comprehensive Sunday collection procedures I developed circa 1990. While I can't say whether the procedures were implemented throughout the archdiocese, it seems that in at least one parish, the two serial number records (bags assigned to the ushers, and bags received by the counters) were either not being prepared or weren't being brought together for comparison each week to ensure that the bags received and opened by the counters bore the same serial numbers as the bags put out for use by the ushers.

Capitalizing on that lapse in procedure, the pastor would surreptitiously open a sealed bag, remove a quantity of cash, reseal the remainder of the collection in a new bag, and forge the ushers' signatures on the new bag. He eventually pled guilty to stealing nearly $200,000. A parishioner who led an audit of the parish finances estimated the actual losses to be as high as $600,000.[29] As noted in Chapter II, this discrepancy can be attributed to the fact that prosecutors typically charge only what they believe they can definitely prove to the satisfaction of a jury; actual losses frequently exceed the amount charged by tens if not hundreds of thousands of dollars.

Once positive control has been established over the collection for a particular Mass or service, that collection is protected from *internal theft* until it is opened for the counting and banking process. The term "internal theft" refers to theft by clergy, staff or other persons having legitimate access to the building in which the collections are stored and processed. Naturally, it is also important to protect the collections from *external theft*, that is, theft by burglars and other opportunists who would not hesitate to steal one or more collection bags if the opportunity presented itself. We know this happens from time to time because of news accounts that almost invariably follow the commission of such thefts. While the existence of external theft is very real, its impact upon church revenue is miniscule in comparison to the impact of internal theft. Suffice it to say, therefore, that ushers should be alert to the potential for sneak thefts during and after church services, and pastors should ensure that collections awaiting the counting and banking process are stored in a locked safe or other locked receptacle until it is time for the counting to begin.

This brings us to the next critical point in a collection's journey from basket to bank: the counting and banking process. Before we get into the details of that, however, a point needs to be made regarding the importance of *total* security. We've all heard the old truism about a chain being only as strong as its weakest link. Well, the same can be said for a security system comprised of multiple components. Those who believe they can discard or dispense with one or more of those components without rendering the entire system flawed are only fooling themselves. A determined thief will zero in on the discarded or inoperative component and exploit it.

Adopting the more visible elements of collection security (serially numbered bags or seals) while discarding or ignoring the less visible elements (witnessing, verifying, etc.) can create a facade or appearance of security behind which a determined embezzler can and will pocket large amounts of cash, usually weekly. Similarly, implementing secure counting and banking procedures without also implementing secure collection procedures is like trying to fill a tub without first closing the drain. When dealing with cash operations, you either are or you aren't secure; there is no in-between!

A Case in Point

On a couple of occasions, I've had the pleasure of implementing at the parish level the Sunday collection procedures I developed. On one such occasion, following my presentation to a parish finance committee, the pastor allowed me to implement the secure collection procedures but, despite all of my pleading, balked at allowing me to implement the companion secure counting and banking procedures. Two years later, following an incident observed and reported to the pastor by his secretary, he called and asked me to implement the missing procedures.

On the first Sunday the secure counting and banking procedures were implemented, the cash portion of that parish's collection jumped several hundred dollars, and it remained elevated from that time on. Comparison of cash receipts for the ensuing year with the comparable period of the prior year revealed an increase totaling roughly $25,000 that could only reasonably be explained by concluding that cash losses sustained during the prior year were no longer occurring due to the presence of secure counting and banking procedures. Easter and Christmas alone accounted for about twenty percent of that figure; while check donations received on those two holy days rose six percent from one year to the next, cash donations rose seventy-six percent, or more than $6,000!

In all probability, the two-year delay in implementing secure counting and banking procedures cost that parish somewhere in the neighborhood of $50,000 in stolen collection funds, and there were strong indications the embezzlement had been in operation for several years preceding my presentation to the finance committee. The individual responsible for those losses was quietly removed but, to my knowledge, the matter was never reported to the local prelate.

Counting and Banking

Among those dioceses that have issued Sunday collection guidelines - however inadequate those guidelines almost invariably prove to be - they almost always reference the need for the counting to be performed by no less than two persons. That instruction alone is a recipe for disaster in the form of repetitive (think *weekly*) theft. With only two counters present, a counter who is so inclined can remove cash from the counting table while the other counter is answering the call of nature, responding to the doorbell, getting a cup of coffee, or attending to some other function that has, even momentarily, taken their focus from the counting table. Because of that potential, no bags or sacks may be opened until at least three counters are present to witness the opening and perform the count.

In order to be reasonably assured that three counters will be available, at least four counters should be scheduled for each week's count. That way, if one of the scheduled counters does not report for duty, the count may still proceed safely. All counters should be totally free of other duties, e.g., answering the telephone or door, preparing meals or performing any other duties. No one should ever be left alone with the collection, not even for five seconds. In addition to being a major breach of security, it also exposes the individual to suspicion in the event of a loss or even a suspected loss.

Each week's count must be documented via standardized forms. Those forms must be designed so that, when completed, they clearly reflect whether or not the required counting and verification procedures were followed. The forms should be reviewed and filed each week by someone not otherwise involved in the counting and banking process. A sample form illustrating the detail needed for currency counting is shown at the end of this chapter. All recording, counting and banking materials should be assembled at the counting table *before* the seals on any bags or sacks are broken.

When it is time to begin the count, all accumulated sacks should be retrieved from the safe or other storage location. A form listing the weekly Masses or services should be used to record the bag or sack serial numbers, thereby ensuring that all collection containers are accounted for each week. Before being opened, each bag or sack must be examined to verify that it was properly sealed. If serially numbered polyethylene bags are used, they should be closely examined for cuts along edges that have been taped or glued. If tamper-proof seals are used, the seal should be checked to ensure it cannot be opened by merely tugging on it, and that it shows no signs of having been forced open and then glued back together. Each bag or seal number should then be recorded on the form.

After all seals have been checked and the serial numbers recorded, the bags or sacks should be opened and emptied onto the table where the cash portion of the collection will be counted. From that point forward, the cash may not be moved to any other location until the counting process has been completed. Before being put aside, each bag or sack should be checked to ensure that it is completely empty.

If numbered seals are used, they must be retained and submitted with all other documentation relating to the count. Similarly, if serially numbered bags are used, they must be retained. Problems such as inadequate sealing, torn sacks or defective seals must be documented and referred to the pastor or other designated person; the seal recording form or a separate form should be used for that purpose. Any such write-up should identify the Mass or service and collection (first or second) involved. Where circumstances such as obvious indications of tampering are noted, the pastor or other appropriate official should be promptly advised of the particulars.

Before any counting takes place, all offering envelopes should be opened and the contents checked against the donor's entry. Any discrepancies must be noted on the envelope. The envelopes should be accumulated for later use in updating each donor's record. That activity (updating donor records) is not an element of the counting and banking process, and should not be performed until that process has been completed.

Immediately after the checks, currency and coin have been separated, at least two counters will remain at the opening table and, independently of each other, count and record the currency on *separate* currency forms. Neither counter may leave the table or perform any other duties until both have completed their counts *and* made a line-by-line verification of their respective figures, resolving any and all differences. Both counters must independently satisfy themselves that the figures are totally accurate. No deductions, exchanges or payments of any type may be made from the collection funds. Such actions are, at best, improper and invariably open the door to theft.

When both currency counters are in agreement, one will record the currency on a bank deposit slip in duplicate. The second counter will verify the entry and, with the first counter, initial the deposit slip and place the original with the currency in a bank deposit bag which will then be locked or sealed. If the count is performed on Sunday, the deposit bag may be taken to the bank's night depository or locked in the rectory safe for overnight retention pending deposit on the first business day of the week. While guidelines are also needed for processing the check and coin portions of collections, it is the paper currency that is far and away most vulnerable to theft in the absence of the guidelines described above.

As a matter of prudent practice, and to maintain depth of experience and versatility, the various duties described above should be rotated on a regular basis. This can best be accomplished by disseminating a monthly or quarterly schedule of counting team assignments. The preparation and dissemination of a schedule also helps counters secure a replacement for unscheduled absences. The larger the pool of counters, the less chance there is for collusion or what might be termed *counter-burnout* due to the same people being tapped for duty every week.

Although the pastor should designate an overall coordinator, narrow specialization or domination of the process by one individual is generally unwise. A complement of broadly trained volunteers will help ensure that key elements of the system do not fall into disuse and thereby cause the system to become vulnerable to theft.

Each week - preferably not later than the day following the counting and banking - the designated verifier will compare the serial numbers of the opened bags or seals against the serial numbers recorded separately by the bag/seal custodian who assigned them to the ushers. If any discrepancies are noted, it is important that the bags or seals be available for examination and use in any follow-up investigation that might be initiated. If no discrepancies are noted, the bags or seals may then be discarded. However, the bag or seal records must be kept on file for at least one year for review by diocesan auditors or other persons responsible for verifying compliance.

As far as the physical equipment needed to establish positive control over a Sunday collection is concerned, mail-type sacks equipped with drawstring and hasp closures have been around since well before 1900, and serially numbered tamper-proof seals have been around for the past one hundred years. More recently, serially numbered, tamper-evident polyethylene bags have come into widespread use. As long as they are properly used, the drawstring sacks and numbered seals are just as effective as the serially numbered bags, but the serially numbered bags do have one advantage over the sack and numbered seal combination: they provide all-in-one security whereas the drawstring sacks require two components (a numbered seal and a drawstring sack) to complete the process.

The decision regarding which of the two systems to use comes down to the judgment of those involved in implementing it. Since the thrust of this book is that the security procedures must be mandated from the highest level of authority, it follows that the decision about which bagging system to use should be made at that level. In no case should the decision be made below the diocesan level. Among other advantages, the bulk purchase of supplies such as serially numbered polyethylene bags or drawstring sacks and numbered seals at the diocesan level can achieve monetary savings that would otherwise be lost.

At first blush, the above-described procedures might strike the average reader as being excessively detailed, but those details are precisely what are needed to create the level of security that must exist in order to establish and maintain a genuinely secure Sunday collection. The objective of this chapter was to establish beyond reasonable doubt that there is essentially only one way to effectively secure a congregation's offerings between basket and bank. It is my hope the reader now recognizes and understands two things:

1.) there is indeed essentially only one way to effectively secure a congregation's offerings between basket and bank, and

2.) the procedures described in this chapter clearly constitute that way.

The next chapter will establish the reasons why the secure procedures described in this chapter must be mandated from the highest level of Church authority in America: the U.S. Conference of Catholic Bishops.

CURRENCY COUNTING FORM

Counter _____   Date _____

Collection   Regular ☐   Special ☐

	1st Bank Deposit (if any)		2nd Bank Deposit		[Cross-total]
Item	# banded bills	Value	# banded bills	Value	# loose bills	Value	Total Value
$1.							
$5							
$10							
$20							
$50							
$100							

Other

Total 1st Deposit $ _____   Value banded $ _____   Value loose $ _____

Total 2nd Deposit $ _____   Value loose $ _____

Total Value All: $ _____   Total 2nd Deposit $ _____   Total Value All $ _____

Note: **Total Value All** shown on left must equal **Total Value All** on right

F-SCform 1/11/03

Chapter V

Why Put the Onus for Reform on the USCCB?

Second on the list of particulars I undertook to establish beyond reasonable doubt is that to have a uniformly efficacious and lasting effect, genuinely secure procedures must be mandated from the highest level of church authority. In the case of the Catholic Church in America, that level is the U.S. Conference of Catholic Bishops (USCCB). While those who possess a background in retail sales will find it self-evident that such procedures be mandated from the highest level, it is perhaps less evident to those who have never been involved in business operations, especially operations involving the receipt and disposal of revenue.

The thought of any retail business with two or more outlets lacking a uniform system for securing its revenue at the point of sale is unthinkable in this day and age, and has been so for the past fifty years or more. Can anyone picture Sears, Penny's or any of the hundreds of other nationwide retailers directing their district managers (let alone individual store managers) to receive and process their sales receipts in whatever manner they see fit? Yet, more than a decade into the twenty-first century, the Catholic Church in America - with just under eighteen thousand parishes[30] (think *retail outlets*) divided between 195 dioceses and archdioceses[31] (think *district offices*) – has, in effect, taken that stand, relying mainly upon trust, happenstance, and the varying judgments of 195 prelates and their financial officers to secure its principal source of income: the Sunday collection.

My journey from ordinary churchgoer to impassioned revenue protection advocate began in 1988 when, as a newly retired member of the Catholic community in the South Region of the Archdiocese of Boston, I attempted to launch a private consulting service specializing in custom-tailored security systems oriented toward revenue protection at the parish level. My *business plan* was to offer individual pastors within the South Region a comprehensive security survey at no cost to the parish. Based upon the results of that survey, the pastor would then have the option of saying "thanks, but no thanks" or, for a very modest fee, enlisting my services to develop and implement a secure system specifically tailored to the needs of his parish.

Before attempting to launch my service, I presented the concept to the then head of the South Region, Most Reverend Daniel A. Hart, who I had worked with on a previous project. Bishop Hart was familiar with my background and, in regard to my business plan, stated in an April 15, 1988 letter: "I think it addresses a real need and I hope you will be successful." As an aside, and with one notable exception detailed later in this book, Bishop Hart was to be the last source of candor I would encounter within the hierarchy.

Having obtained Bishop Hart's approval, including permission to use his name in my written approach to individual pastors, I then developed an information packet and transmittal letter offering to conduct a security survey at no cost or obligation to the parish. Each mailing piece was addressed to the pastor by name, marked "Personal" and included a personalized transmittal letter, a tri-fold brochure, a reply form, and a pre-addressed reply envelope. Following is the text of my transmittal letter.

P.S. SERVICES
Post Office Box 475
Canton, MA 02021-0475

PERSONAL
Rev. [pastor's name]
[parish name]
[street address]   May 26, 1988
[town, state, zip]

Dear Rev. [last name]:

In your role as a pastor, you've probably wondered, at one time or another, whether your Sunday offering is being handled in the most secure manner possible. As we both know, the process of making that determination is somewhat complicated and sensitized by the presence of a volunteer work force.

Assuming you have pondered the level of security presently afforded your offering but haven't followed through, for whatever reason (lack of a security resource, possible affront to workers, lack of a <u>known</u> problem, etc.), you'll find the enclosed brochure most interesting. If you inherited your present system, you owe it to yourself to give this brochure a close reading.

Fixed responsibility is the nucleus of any reliable system for protecting employees as well as funds. When responsibility is not fixed, unexplained and often undetected losses are likely to occur. While I don't mean to imply that your staff cannot or should not be trusted, I believe you'd agree the economic well-being of your parish is too important to hinge on trust alone. Sound business principles and practices are essential.

As information, Fr. [last name], I provided samples of this packet to Bishop Hart and Chancellor [name withheld], and was subsequently advised that the Archdiocese employs an individual whose duties include internal audit and assets security. As I understand it, this individual will visit any parish having a problem that requires special attention. Please note, however, we evaluate systems to identify and correct weaknesses <u>before</u> they become problems that require "special attention".

If you decide a survey of your Sunday offering system just might be judicious, simply complete the enclosed request form and mail it in the envelope provided. I will call you to arrange a mutually agreeable date and time at which we can meet to discuss, <u>without obligation</u>, your present system and procedures.

Sincerely,

Michael W. Ryan
President

To my great surprise, of the nearly one hundred packets I mailed to pastors within the South Region, I didn't receive a single reply. Not one pastor opted to take advantage of my offer of a free security survey each of them knew had their bishop's endorsement. This was a real eye-opener. I realized for the first time that, by and large, pastors are unwilling to subject their security procedures and, by inference, their revenue handling procedures to outside scrutiny regardless of how well intentioned or potentially beneficial that scrutiny might be.

Having been rebuffed at the parish level, I then turned my attention to the next level of authority, the Archdiocese of Boston, then under the direction of Bernard Cardinal Law. However, after several unsuccessful attempts to convince the Cardinal and his chancellor of the absolute need for secure Sunday collection procedures, and because the Archdiocese of Boston was and remains only one of 195 archdioceses and dioceses spread across the fifty states, I concluded my efforts should be redirected to the top of the Church's hierarchical pyramid in America which, at that time (1990) was the National Conference of Catholic Bishops (NCCB). Since then, and although I became absolutely convinced that needed change must flow from the very top, I nevertheless periodically importuned Cardinal Law and, subsequently, Sean Cardinal O'Malley to implement secure Sunday collection procedures within the Archdiocese of Boston. Unfortunately, all of my urgings fell upon seemingly deaf ears.

A basic and unofficial chart depicting the organizational structure of the U.S. Catholic Church is shown on the next page. The purpose of the chart is to provide a framework for the reader to more easily assimilate all of the correspondence, particularly that contained in the next two chapters and appendix. Between the chart and the correspondence, it should be apparent to readers that I reached out to every level of the hierarchy in a very substantial way in my efforts to convince the hierarchy of the urgent need for corrective measures.

Clearly, needed change cannot originate at the parish level. It is sheer insanity to expect that each of nearly eighteen thousand pastors either is or should be capable of figuring out how to effectively secure their collections from basket to bank and at all points in between. In the same vein, it is unrealistic to expect 195 archdioceses and dioceses to independently accomplish that same objective, especially since we learned from the previous chapter there is really only one way to effectively secure a Sunday collection system.

Basic Hierarchical Structure of the Catholic Church in America

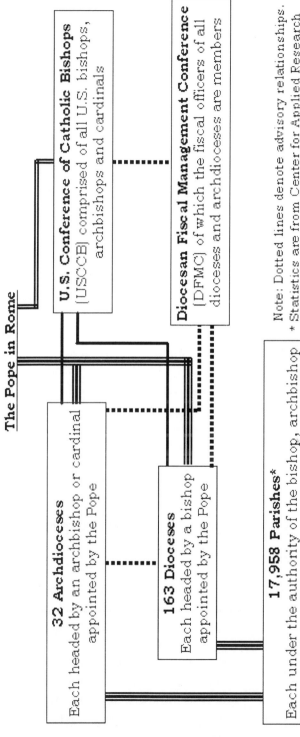

The Pope in Rome

U.S. Conference of Catholic Bishops
(USCCB) comprised of all U.S. bishops, archbishops and cardinals

Diocesan Fiscal Management Conference
(DFMC) of which the fiscal officers of all dioceses and archdioceses are members

32 Archdioceses
Each headed by an archbishop or cardinal appointed by the Pope

163 Dioceses
Each headed by a bishop appointed by the Pope

17,958 Parishes*
Each under the authority of the bishop, archbishop or cardinal in whose jurisdiction the parish exists. As a group, they serve **65.6 million Catholics***

Note: Dotted lines denote advisory relationships.
* Statistics are from Center for Applied Research in the Apostolate, http://cara.georgetown.edu/ CARAServices/requestedchurchstats.html 2010

In Chapter III, I cited an article published in the Archdiocese of Milwaukee's weekly newspaper, *Catholic Herald*. Entitled "Church embezzlement is theft, but also betrayal of trust."[32] Readers will recall that article highlighted two Sunday collection embezzlement cases and explored the area of causative factors. The first case involved a parish bookkeeper's embezzlement of more than $500,000, and the second involved a parish volunteer's embezzlement of more than $300,000. The article's subtitle read, "Internal financial controls key to preventing loss."[33] Readers will also recall from Chapter I that the Association of Certified Fraud Examiners (ACFE) identified the lack of adequate internal controls as being the most commonly cited factor that allowed fraud to occur.

As implied by the article's subtitle, and according to the director of Milwaukee's Archdiocesan Office for Parish Finances, much of the blame for those two embezzlements was attributed to "inadequate parish internal controls to prevent theft." The director went on to declare that "the Office for Parish Finances created a parish financial management manual which gives parishes guidelines for proper financial controls," and that there is a section on internal controls that "addresses all financial controls, including cash handling procedures."[34] Readers who compare the Milwaukee archdiocese's cash handling procedures ("Collection Receipts Procedures"[35]) with the procedures described in Chapter IV will quickly recognize the archdiocese's procedures are inadequate. Following are the Sunday collection guidelines provided by the Archdiocese in their parish financial management manual:

5.6 **Collection Receipts Procedures.** Collections refer to cash or check contributions received from general parish collections during church services or meetings. The following procedures will help to ensure the integrity of this major source of parish revenue.

5.6.1 Loose cash and envelopes should be collected by ushers during the service and should be taken immediately to a secure location. If the collection basket is placed at the altar as part of a presentation of gifts at the Offertory, two individuals should be assigned to remove this basket after the distribution of communion and take the basket to the secure location. The collection may be counted immediately following the mass, or it may be counted on the first workday after the weekend. The entire unsorted collection should be placed in tamper-proof bags and stored in a locked, fireproof safe, or placed in the bank night depository, until it is counted. The collection should remain in view of at least two individuals at all times.

5.6.2 At least two unrelated people should be present when cash is counted after collections. Signed count sheets or logs should be maintained.

5.6.3 When counting collections, loose collections should be counted separately from those received in envelopes. This will facilitate the reconciliation of the envelope amount at a later time.

5.6.4 The counters should restrictively endorse ("For Deposit Only in the Account of _____") all checks received in the collections.

5.6.5 As amounts received in envelopes are counted, the amount should be recorded on the face of the envelope.

5.6.6 The counters should prepare a deposit slip and all amounts should be deposited in the bank deposit vault immediately after all collections for the day are completed. Any amounts not deposited shall be kept in a locked fireproof safe.

5.6.7 Envelopes and count sheets should be forwarded to the parish bookkeeper. The bookkeeper should record the deposit in the parish checkbook or ledgers.

5.6.8 The bookkeeper should post identifiable contributions (i.e., envelope users) to each parishioner's individual record. The bookkeeper should also reconcile the amounts posted to the envelope amount plus loose collections indicated on the deposit slip.

5.6.9 Individuals performing the counting should be rotated on a regular basis. There should be an odd number of teams consisting of at least 3 unrelated persons on each team. No team should be allowed to count the same week each month.[36]

Milwaukee's guidelines are a typical example of the hit-and-run treatment afforded Sunday collection security by the majority of dioceses and archdioceses. Section 5.6.1, for example, attempts to incorporate into one 125-word paragraph procedures that require several hundred words to adequately explain. The result is a disjointed, non-sequential, illogical and wholly inadequate instruction.

Take a moment to read that section again. The guidelines are missing several of the key elements needed to ensure that no one, not even the pastor, has lone, unobserved access to the collections between their collection by the ushers and their deposit into the parish bank account. Among the missing elements are the act of positively securing the collection at the first opportunity (when the ushers meet to consolidate their baskets), the use of serially numbered bags or sack seals, and the requirement that at least three counters be present for the counting process. Each of those missing elements is an unintended yet clear invitation to weekly theft.

So here we have an archdiocese identifying the problem ("inadequate parish internal controls") in 2004 but, fully seven years later, still failing to provide the level of detailed guidance parishes must have in order to prevent Sunday collection embezzlements. Did the director and her staff formulate and issue guidelines they knew were clearly inadequate? I don't believe so. The problem, I believe, lies in the fact that neither the director nor her staff are sufficiently familiar with or fully understand the elements that *must* be present to establish and maintain a genuinely secure Sunday collection system. I sincerely doubt that even ten percent of the 195 dioceses possess the necessary expertise. Whether they do or they don't, however, we know from the last chapter there is essentially only one way to ensure the integrity of the collections, thus rendering pointless any endeavor to formulate guidelines on a diocese-by-diocese basis.

In a relevant aside, it is worth noting the above guidelines were issued in 2009 under the administration of then Milwaukee Archbishop Timothy M. Dolan who, in addition to being elected President of the USCCB in 2010, now heads the Archdiocese of New York and is no doubt well on his way to becoming a cardinal. In a letter to me dated December 10, 2010, Archbishop Dolan stated:

> I could not agree with you more that the (arch)bishops of the United States need to take every precaution in their (arch)dioceses to ensure that Sunday and holy day collections are not tampered with by anyone. Here in the archdiocese, we have a locked-box arrangement, which makes it nearly impossible for anyone to get near the collections. While I will be sure to mention this matter to the bishops through the conference, this is, as you have been told, not something over which the conference has jurisdiction. <u>The conference does not have the right to interfere with a bishop's administration of his diocese other than by enforcing the directives approved by the Holy See.</u>

(emphasis added)

Archbishop Dolan's letter was in response to a letter I sent to him, urging that the USCCB act under the empowering provisions of Canon 455 to implement secure collection procedures conference-wide. As can be seen from Archbishop Dolan's reply, he blithely ignored my reference to Canon 455. In the next chapter, you will see this tactic - ignore what cannot be refuted – repeatedly employed by various members of the hierarchy.

There is another factor that militates against leaving the matter of Sunday collection security up to the varied opinions and judgments of 195 prelates and their staffs. I mentioned in the last chapter that the Archdiocese of Chicago codified and disseminated my guidelines in 2005, the assumption being that those guidelines would be and were implemented archdiocese-wide. Imagine my surprise, therefore, when my nephew, an up-and-coming Chicago attorney who I had asked to make a few observations at Holy Name Cathedral, reported back to me that on two Sundays in early 2011, the collections for the Masses he attended were not positively secured (as required by Chicago's own guidelines) when the ushers met at the rear of the cathedral to consolidate the collection. Instead, the ushers' baskets were merely dumped into a larger basket that was then transported down a stairway and out of sight. In one instance, the transporting usher was not accompanied by anyone. As the reader will recall from the last chapter, failure to positively secure the collection concurrent with the consolidation of the ushers' baskets is a major breach of the secure procedures.

As the seat of the Archdiocese of Chicago, one would expect Holy Name Cathedral to serve as a model for how all other churches within the archdiocese should function. Well, that's what one would think if there weren't other factors to be considered. For example, did Cardinal George or the pastor decide it is unseemly or inappropriate to secure the collection in a location within the cathedral where that procedure might be observed by one or more parishioners? Did one or more of the ushers become indignant and play the "You don't trust us!" card? Was the procedure dispensed with by the pastor or head usher as being (in their eyes) unnecessary? Whatever the reason(s), it is clear someone felt comfortable discarding a crucial element of the secure collection procedures, no doubt in part because it is *only* a diocesan directive and therefore subject to modification by diocesan personnel. Bottom line, the collections at the cardinal's own church are exposed to weekly thefts because someone - who might or might not have a hidden agenda - felt comfortable making a decision to dispense with an essential element of the system.

This example of ignoring archdiocese-issued guidelines supports my contention that such guidelines must be issued by the USCCB. If there is any area of operation within the Catholic Church (or any other denomination that collects cash donations during its services) that cries out to be standardized, it is the manner in which each parish receives, holds, processes and deposits its congregation's weekly donations. Diocesan personnel are far less likely to ignore or contravene guidelines issued by the USCCB, particularly since such guidelines will also bear the *imprimatur* of the Vatican.

The reason given by the USCCB for their failure to issue guidelines for Conference-wide implementation has been their contention they are not empowered by Canon Law to decree how individual bishops must handle the collections within their respective dioceses. Strictly speaking, that is correct. But what they refuse to acknowledge is the fact that Canon Law provides a means whereby they can become empowered to issue such a decree.

The reality, then, is that the USCCB, for reasons best known to its leadership, does not wish to be canonically empowered in this matter. Were they to be so empowered, they would then be obligated to issue a general decree mandating conference-wide implementation of genuinely secure procedures for the Church's principal source of income: the Sunday collections. From the various communications contained in the next and succeeding chapters, you will see that the objective of securing the Church's principal source of revenue is conspicuously missing from the USCCB's priorities.

While I neither have nor claim to have expertise in Canon Law, I can read and understand clear writing and will leave it to the reader to decide whether the Canon Law I have cited in my correspondence with the hierarchy applies as I have insisted it does. In that regard, however, I erred initially in citing Canon 1265 §2 from a version prepared by the Canon Law Society Of Great Britain and Ireland, not realizing there is some variance between that version and the version prepared by the Canon Law Society of America and approved by the then National Conference of Catholic Bishops. In the former version (Great Britain and Ireland), that canon reads as follows:

> The Episcopal Conference can draw up rules regarding collections, which must be observed by all, including those who from their foundation are called and are 'mendicants'.[37] (emphasis added)

My elation at finding such a seemingly clear statement was short lived, however, when I discovered in a subsequent review of the version prepared by the Canon Law Society of America that Canon 1265 §2 reads as follows:

> The conference of bishops can establish norms for begging for alms which all must observe, including those who by their foundation are called and are mendicants.[38] (emphasis added)

I mention this detour in my search for documentation because Canon 1265 §2 is mentioned in my correspondence with one or more prelates and USCCB officials. And while not one of them took exception to its use, I want the reader to understand that my referencing Canon 1265 §2 was a misstep. Fortunately, I eventually discovered Canon 455 which reads as follows:

> §1 A conference of bishops can only issue general decrees in cases where universal law has prescribed it or a special mandate of the Apostolic See has established it either *motu proprio* or at the request of the conference itself.
>
> §2. The decrees mentioned in §1, in order to be enacted validly in a plenary meeting, must be passed by at least a two-thirds vote of the prelates who belong to the conference and possess a deliberative vote. They do not obtain binding force unless they have been legitimately promulgated after having been reviewed by the Apostolic See.
>
> §3. The conference of bishops itself determines the manner of promulgation and the time when the decrees take effect.
>
> §4. In cases in which neither universal law nor a special mandate of the Apostolic See has granted the power mentioned in §1 to a conference of bishops, the competence of each diocesan bishop remains intact, nor is a conference or its president able to act in the name of all the bishops unless each and every bishop has given consent.[39]

Clearly, Canon 455 provides conferences the means to become empowered to issue general decrees. As a matter of fact, the USCCB has availed itself of that canon's authorizing mechanism on a number of occasions since Pope John Paul II promulgated the revised Code of Canon Law in 1983. In the USCCB's own words:

> This website contains a compilation of the complementary norms approved by the United States Conference of Catholic Bishops. In some instances the bishops voted to retain existing norms or regulations, with due regard for any change or modification warranted by changes in the revised code; in other instances they revised existing norms or created new norms where necessary. <u>Those actions requiring recognitio or approval from the Apostolic See in accord with canon 455§2 have been reviewed by the appropriate Roman dicastery.</u>[40] (emphasis added)

The USCCB's steadfast refusal to utilize the empowering provisions of Canon 455 to effectively protect the Church's principal source of income is therefore all the more baffling, strongly suggesting the presence of paralyzing fear, a hidden agenda or both.

What does the USCCB have to fear? Only they know for sure, and they're not talking. But possible causes that come to mind include, first and foremost, fear that the Conference-wide implementation of genuinely secure procedures would result in the more or less simultaneous discovery of multiple embezzlements within many dioceses and archdioceses, thereby triggering a new spate of negative publicity at a time when the bishops (in their minds, at least) are just beginning to stitch together the tattered remnants of their once positive image as the premier arbiters of moral and ethical standards of conduct.

The irony of that head-in-the-sand stance, however, is that by refusing to acknowledge the systemic nature of Sunday collection embezzlements and to address that malady on a Conference-wide basis, the USCCB is repeating the colossal error that allowed the sexual abuse scourge to last <u>decades</u> longer than it should have. The damage to innocent lives was far worse than it would have been had the USCCB responded correctly when that scourge was first brought credibly to their attention.

The bishops, as represented by the USCCB, are on record as claiming they learned from their grievous mishandling of the abuse scandal,[41] yet here they are nearly ten years later obstinately denying the obvious (that collection thefts are a systemic, Church-wide problem) and washing their hands of any responsibility for correcting it.

A close second to the fear of negative publicity, I believe, is the fear that the USCCB would not be able to secure the assent of two-thirds of the prelates to take action in the matter, as required by Section 2 of Canon 455. As you will recall from Chapter IV, there is really only one way to effectively secure the Sunday collections. Consequently, expected "nay" votes cannot be a matter of some bishops wishing to secure their dioceses' collections in a different yet somehow equally effective manner. Diocesan prelates answer to no one but the Pope, and they are unwilling to cede any portion of their authority to anyone, including the USCCB to which they all belong. Just think what a public relations disaster that would be. Picture the headlines: "U.S. Bishops Refuse to Protect Church's Primary Source of Income" or words to that effect.

If I were a betting man, my money would be on the two considerations noted above – fear of negative publicity arising from the simultaneous discovery of numerous embezzlements, and fear of failing to obtain the approval of two thirds of the bishops - as the main reasons why the USCCB has not sought Vatican approval to implement genuinely secure procedures conference-wide.

Another possible cause of the USCCB's failure to act is the fear of a *rebellion* among clergy suddenly denied access to a ready source of supplemental income. Other causative factors might be formulated and put forth as justification for their inaction, but none of those factors are or ever can be valid. While it helps to have some sense of the most likely reasons for the USCCB's nonfeasance, none of those reasons change the fact that it is nonfeasance and will remain so unless and until the USCCB does what ought to be done to protect the Church's primary source of income.

In the next chapter, you will have an opportunity to see how the USCCB has bobbed and weaved around the issue of Sunday collection security and their role in its development and implementation. Their responses to questions and statements relating to the Church's main source of income provide insight into their motives and the lengths to which they will go to avoid their obvious responsibility to act in this matter.

Chapter VI

The USCCB's Decades-Old Failure to Act

*They tie up heavy burdens
and lay them on people's shoulders,
but they will not lift a finger to move them.*
Matthew 23:4

Third on the list of particulars I undertook to establish beyond reasonable doubt is that the hierarchy of the Roman Catholic Church in America has intentionally shunned Church-wide implementation of readily available, low-cost, genuinely secure procedures that, properly implemented and monitored, would end virtually all currently ongoing Sunday collection embezzlements, and prevent virtually all future such embezzlements as well as the sins that attach to *and* flow from those acts.

If my efforts to cause the hierarchy to implement truly secure procedures Church-wide can be viewed as a call for reform (I believe they can be), the words of noted Catholic Theologian Avery Cardinal Dulles (1918-2008) would appear to apply. In an essay adapted from a lecture delivered at Fordham University, Cardinal Dulles stated:

> In any discussion of reform, two opposite errors are to be avoided. The first is to assume that because the Church is divinely instituted, it never needs to be reformed. This position is erroneous because it fails to attend to the human element. Since all the members of the Church, including the Pope and the bishops, are limited in virtue and ability, they may fail to live up to the principles of the faith itself. When guilty of negligence, timidity, or misjudgment, they may need to be corrected, as Paul, for example, corrected Peter (Galatians 2:11). The second error would be to assail or undermine the essentials of Catholic Christianity. This would not be reform but dissolution.[42] (emphasis added)

Note that Cardinal Dulles recognized the hierarchy can be "guilty of negligence" *and* that they "may need to be corrected." The latter remark raises this question: By whom can the Pope and the bishops be corrected? Cardinal Dulles provided the answer a bit further into his lecture when he stated:

> Within the Church itself, the laity have certain rights and responsibilities, as sharers by baptism in the threefold office of Christ, prophet, priest, and king. Their talents should be used for the benefit of the Church. Although the order of the Catholic Church cannot be congregational, members of the congregation can make a positive contribution, especially where their professional skills and experience are needed. There is every reason why the voice of the faithful should be heard, provided it does not come from an adversarial stance as part of a scheme to seize power.[43] (emphasis added)

I trust at this juncture - or at least before reaching the end of this book - the reader will have recognized that this call for Church-wide measures to truly protect the Church's primary source of income can in no way, shape or form be considered "a scheme to seize power." Rather, it is simply and solely intended "for the benefit of the Church."

In thinking about how much of my correspondence this book must contain in order to establish the hierarchy's nonfeasance, I vacillated about whether I should include all of it or whether the case could be made using only selected pieces of correspondence. In the interest of clarity and in order to maintain the focus of attention where it belongs, I decided to be selective, using mainly correspondence directed to and received from USCCB presidents and other prelates. In addition, the bulk of that correspondence has been placed in an appendix so that those readers who find my summaries sufficient and would rather not read each letter are not forced to do so.

Responses from USCCB staff members, while of interest, reflect the staff members' interpretation of the policy or position they were instructed to transmit. This is in contrast to the replies of the Conference presidents and other prelates that provide some insight into the leaders' personal opinions and motives. Still, I found it necessary to include staff correspondence in some instances wherein the prelate chose not to reply.

I should also note that in the evolution of my focus from the parish and diocesan level to the national level, what little for-profit motivation I had gradually dissipated. By the time I began corresponding with Church officials at the national level, my for-profit motivation had pretty much ended. If I had to put my finger on the turning point, I would say it was the day my youngest son – after hearing me complain for the umpteenth time about the general lack of interest in collection security at the parish level – asked, "Dad, is your objective to make money or cause change?" It was then I realized two things: my son has a gift for seeing to the heart of a matter, and the chances of my convincing the hierarchy of the urgent need for fundamental change would be hampered, perhaps even defeated, by the presence of any element of recompense.

Early in my consistently unproductive correspondence with diocesan officials, most notably those of the Archdiocese of Boston, I thought there must be some aspect of the Sunday collection security issue I was not articulating well enough to cause or allow them to see the Sunday collections' extreme vulnerability and the absolute need for corrective measures emanating from the diocesan level. I tried to give them the benefit of the doubt, but it eventually dawned on me that, by and large, they did then and do now understand the issue. Yet, for one or more of the reasons discussed at the end of Chapter V, or for reasons I have yet to divine, they steadfastly refused to admit it. Consequently, by the time I began writing to NCCB (now USCCB) officials, I was already half expecting to receive the runaround and, in that, they did not disappoint. I mention this because some of my letters contain an element of frustration or sharpness that won't be lost on the reader.

In many instances, the hierarchy's communications are remarkable for what they do not contain. Indeed, a number of prelates and other USCCB officials refused to even acknowledge receipt of my correspondence. While they were certainly free to ignore me, I believe their decision to do so says something about their integrity. A numerical summary of the correspondence I've had with the hierarchy at every level of the U.S. Catholic Church is shown on the next page.

I also corresponded with the Holy See on two occasions, eliciting a response in both instances. Those letters appear later in this chapter. While I have also corresponded with a number of pastors over the years, that correspondence is not relevant to the central issue (the hierarchy's failure to act) and is therefore being omitted.

Regarding the USCCB, I am convinced they have in place an unwritten, never-to-be-admitted variation of the old *divide and conquer* strategy. That strategy is very simple, the principal element being for the USCCB to convince all who inquire that the USCCB is not canonically empowered and, <u>by inference</u>, cannot become canonically empowered to direct how their member prelates must handle the collections within their respective dioceses.

As long as the USCCB can keep responsibility for the protection of the Church's principal source of revenue out of their lap and in the laps of 195 individual prelates, the USCCB will never have to address the issue and each prelate will remain free to act or (what is far more likely) not act as he wishes. If you think about it, you will come to realize that strategy, although diabolical in nature and highly destructive in its effects, is quite clever in its simplicity and has worked perfectly for decades, even generations!

Numerical Summary of Correspondence To and From the U.S. Catholic Hierarchy
April 13, 1988 through March 4, 2011

	Letters Sent	Replies Received From Addressee	Replies Received From Subordinate	First and Last Date of Contact
USCCB Presidents (8)	19	4 (21%)	5 (26%)	Nov. 13, 1990 Dec. 30, 2010
USCCB Officials	18	8 (44%)	N/A	Jan. 17, 1990 Mar. 17, 2003
DFMC Presidents	2	-0-	-0-	Jan. 11, 1994 Feb. 22, 2009
DFMC Officials	6*	2 (33%)	N/A	Apr. 17, 1990 Mar. 4, 2011
Archdiocese of Boston	42	27 (64%)	N/A	Apr. 13, 1988 Apr. 4, 2008

* Two of the six were emails sent to members of the Board, 13 on the first occasion and 14 on the second. Except for the correspondence had with the Archdiocese of Boston, many of the letters referenced above are contained in the Appendix.

MWR/5-25-11

Criminal investigators often experience a *smoking-gun* epiphany when they uncover a particular piece of evidence that convinces them the target of their investigation is indeed guilty, and that all that remains is to bring the individual to account for their crime. In this case, however, the target is not an individual but rather an association of individuals. Still, I'll be very surprised if the vast majority of readers do not experience that type of epiphany before reaching the end of this chapter, especially if they also review a representative number of letters contained in the Appendix. In any event, I feel confident in predicting that no reader will reach the end of this chapter believing the USCCB's nonfeasance either is or could be due to a lack of information.

In Chapter V, I mentioned having worked with Bishop Daniel A. Hart, and I said that, with one exception, he was to be the last source of candor I would encounter within the hierarchy. Call it happenstance or destiny but, whatever it was, my first contact (p.108) with the NCCB (now USCCB) occurred in January of 1990 and proved to be the second and final source of candor I would encounter within the hierarchy. To top it off, the individual was not a clergyman but rather a nun, Sister Frances Mlocek, the then NCCB Director of Finance. While I said in the Preface I would not include the names of any persons below the level of bishop, I'm making an exception in this case because I hold Sister Mlocek in high regard and wish to acknowledge my appreciation for her candor.

Sister Mlocek responded promptly, stating that collection security is a matter she had thought about from time to time, although not in quite the same light as I presented it. Sister Mlocek referred my letter and enclosures to the Administrator of the Diocesan Fiscal Management Conference (DFMC) with a transmittal stating that what I proposed was "a very simple solution to a concern that I think many parishes face in the proper handling of their Sunday collections." The DFMC is an offshoot of the USCCB (then NCCB), providing a forum for diocesan fiscal managers to come together and discuss issues and concerns with a view toward developing standard approaches to common fiscal issues and operations.

Sister Mlocek's recommendation and two follow-up letters notwithstanding, the DFMC Administrator failed to provide even the courtesy of an acknowledgment. In spite of the fact that the topic of security for the Church's primary source of income should have captured his attention, it had quite the opposite effect: he and other DFMC officials to whom I subsequently wrote exhibited no interest whatsoever. They were certainly free to ignore me but, like those prelates who opted not to respond to my communications, the fact that they chose that option does not speak well of them or their professional ethics. The DFMC's role in maintaining the unacceptable status quo will be examined in greater detail in the next chapter.

My next approach was made in November of 1990 to the then NCCB President, Archbishop Daniel E. Pilarczyk. It was my first approach (p.110) to a Conference president and included a reference to my failed attempts to convince Cardinal Law of the need to implement genuinely secure procedures within the Archdiocese of Boston. Archbishop Pilarczyk did not reply, opting instead to refer the matter to the NCCB's General Counsel who advised in a letter dated December 10, 1990 that he was confident the Archdiocese of Boston "will be responding to your concerns directly," and that they (Boston) are "in the best position to respond" to the issues I raised. The President's handling of my letter (which clearly pointed out the nationwide nature of the collection security issue) was the first high-level indication of how unwilling the NCCB (now USCCB), its officers and members, were (and remain) to address the issue of Sunday collection security.

Between late 1990 and my first communication with Archbishop Pilarczyk's successor, I corresponded with various prelates including Archbishop Thomas J. Murphy, then Chairman of the NCCB Committee on Stewardship. In my letter (p.111) to Archbishop Murphy, I spoke of the highly vulnerable nature of the average Sunday collection and how that adversely reflects upon the Catholic Church's stewardship. I included a case history and urged him and his committee to "acknowledge and confront this formidable and ongoing drain on Church revenue."

In a reply dated December 9, 1992, Archbishop Murphy stated, "I will bring your concern to the attention of the Ad Hoc Committee to seek their wisdom and insight regarding this matter. Thank you for writing to me."

In retrospect, I noted that Archbishop Murphy, did not acknowledge the subject of my letter (Sunday collection security and embezzlements), only referring to it in his reply as "this matter." With a view toward emphasizing the importance of the issue, I sent him a follow-up letter (p.114). In that letter, I reiterated my concern for the collections' extreme vulnerability, and provided a concrete example of how the implementation of genuinely secure procedures reversed a particular parish's cash flow from being 8.5 percent under the same period of the prior year to 15 percent over the prior year in just seven months time. I ended my letter by offering to collaborate with him and his committee in the development of genuinely secure collection procedures.

Archbishop Murphy replied within a few weeks, stating, in pertinent part:

> It would seem to me that your concern and interest regarding the security of the Sunday collection is an issue which goes beyond the responsibility of our Ad Hoc Committee. It seems to be an issue which would be of interest to Diocesan Fiscal Officers. I know that there is a National Organization of people who hold this position. Moreover, any decision made in this regard is made at the diocesan level.

Although I would write to Archbishop Murphy on two occasions in 1994 in his capacity as Chairman of the NCCB Committee on Budget and Finance, I never heard from him again.

At the diocesan level, I wrote to Cardinal Law on ten occasions between 1988 and 1997, virtually all concerning Sunday collection security. Surprisingly, and to his credit, he personally replied in several instances. In a letter dated March 19, 1993, Cardinal Law declared, "I am quite conscious of fiduciary responsibility, and the fiduciary responsibility of the Church." Of course, I was seeking more than mere consciousness. I was seeking action!

Following is the sixth letter I directed to Cardinal Law; I am including it in the body of this chapter to illustrate that I did everything but draw diagrams to cause him to acknowledge and respond to the Sunday collection's extreme vulnerability.

[letterhead]

November 20, 1992

PERSONAL AND CONFIDENTIAL
Bernard Cardinal Law
Archbishop of Boston
2121 Commonwealth Avenue
Boston, MA 02135

Dear Cardinal Law:

This refers to my October 27 letter regarding the Church's failure to implement effective systems and procedures to protect its greatest source of revenue: the Sunday collection. The lead story for the November 6 issue of The Pilot would seem to underscore the timeliness of my communication. At the risk of wearing out any "welcome" due me, I would therefore like to offer further relevant commentary. I'll be as succinct as possible, consistent with the crucial nature of this subject.

In a well-known fairy tale, it took an innocent child to make the emperor accept the fact that he was parading about in his undergarments. The Church's revenue crisis is no fairy tale and I'm certainly no innocent child, but the Sunday collection is essentially "naked" in virtually every parish in your Archdiocese and, I believe, every other diocese throughout the Unites States. The role of Emperor in this real life tale of fiscal woe is being played by you and your brother Cardinals, Bishops and pastors. The question is: How long will it take for this group of emperors to admit the Sunday collection is defenseless and under attack?

I'll tell you what I've concluded at this point, Eminence. The hierarchy knows the Sunday collection is vulnerable to theft, but doesn't want to end the ability of pastors to access those funds prior to their documentation and official deposit. After all, aren't Roman Catholic priests the least well paid among their peers in other faiths? Shouldn't we give them some way to discreetly supplement their meager income, some means of meeting unexpected and/or special needs? Of course we should - NOT!! You don't bore a hole in the Hoover Dam because you want a drink of water, and you don't expose the Sunday collection to theft by numerous individuals because you wish to accommodate one or two!

In an October 31 Boston Globe article, you are quoted as saying parish revenue decreased four million dollars last year. What percent of that decrease is the result of increased theft? Before you answer reflexively in the negative, be advised it's a question neither you, nor I, nor Chancellor [name withheld], nor anyone else is in a position to answer - especially in the negative! You see, if you haven't implemented secure systems and procedures to signal and deter theft (you haven't), it's impossible to know how much is being lost. But the law of averages and statistical probability (not to mention diocesan and parish files) tell us criminal theft is occurring, and I believe it's happening in many more parishes than anyone has yet surmised. No one can seriously claim it isn't happening; that stance flies in the face of logic.

The following account may be of some interest to you. It's about a suburban parish whose Sunday collection was running about 3% <u>under</u> SPLY for the first 3 months of this calendar year; that is fairly consistent with your data for the diocese as a whole. Anyway, the pastor of this particular parish decided to implement an off-the-shelf collection security system, mainly to placate a local zealot who insisted the collection was highly vulnerable to theft. Well, beginning with start-up day on the first Sunday of April, a very striking turnaround began.

As of the end of October, the collection was averaging about 8% <u>over</u> SPLY and <u>cash</u>, which was running 8.5% <u>under</u> SPLY, tallied more than 15% <u>over</u> SPLY for the 7-month period ending October 31! There could be more than one explanation for this phenomenon - perhaps an unusual variable was not factored in - but a rise of only 4% in check donations (they were even with SPLY for Jan-Mar) while cash donations went from 8.5% <u>under</u> to more than 15% <u>over</u> SPLY, makes it hard to avoid the obvious conclusion. And I know one pastor who wouldn't dream of returning to the old "system." Do your files reflect similar turnarounds sans security measures?

The Globe article also mentioned the option of imposing a tax on parish incomes, but went on to term it "anathema" among "Boston clerics". And you are quoted as characterizing such a tax as "the last and least desirable" way of increasing revenues. All these years, I thought a portion of what I give locally goes toward support of diocesan operations. Isn't that correct? If it is, what's wrong with increasing it? Is it that you perceive those "Boston clerics", one way or another, would reject such a program? Or is your reluctance instead rooted in empathy? If we're not protecting the main source of parish revenue (clearly, we're not) any such empathy is both vacuous and misplaced.

Both the Pilot and Globe articles allude to the formation of committees to study the Archdiocese's mission, revenue, expenses and real estate. I understand Cardinal Bernardin closed some 50 churches and schools in his archdiocese last year. Might your Real Estate Committee recommend closing churches or schools based upon declining revenues? Have you charged your Revenue

Committee with determining whether Sunday collection funds are adequately protected from covert theft? Will the Revenue Committee opt for the convenient approach of recommending that you ask the flock to give more, even though it is (or should be) abundantly clear you are not providing even a minimally acceptable level of protection to what we already give?

Here's a question your finance experts can sink their teeth into: Will our collection system make it into the 20th Century before we enter the 21st? You must know we're still in the 19th Century on the matter of collection security, Eminence. Can you imagine Sears or Penny's handling their income the way the Church does? Who has the most "retail" outlets, they or we? I'll bet we do! If they operated like the Church does in this area, their retail clerks would be transacting sales out of used cigar boxes! That should disturb you and your brother Bishops, Eminence, but apparently it doesn't. All of my efforts to date have been for naught. Has anyone else ever dared to sound the alarm? Will it take a Reverend [name withheld]-like fiasco before anyone wakes up?

I hate to appear like a know-it-all, because that's not me. I'm sure [name withheld] and one or more members of his staff could run circles around me as regards the formalities of accounting. But I do know Internal Security. It's an area of competence for me, one I can only assume no one on your staff possesses. If anyone does, they are either not in a position to apply it, or have perceived (or been advised) that such input is not desired. Whatever the case, I would be remiss if I failed to recapitulate for you what it takes to make a collection secure.

> Before a Sunday collection system can be deemed adequately secure, appropriate security equipment and procedures must be applied so that no one - not even the pastor - has lone, unobserved and undetectable access to those funds. Further, this mantle of protection must begin immediately after the collection is taken up (when it's consolidated at the rear of the church) and must remain absolutely unbroken until it has been properly deposited in the parish bank account.

I'm not sure when it happened, Eminence, but it appears our Church has become a collection of kingdoms (more than 400 in this Archdiocese alone) headed by men, many of whom seem motivated more by an attitude of ownership than one of stewardship. You could call it the "THIS IS MY PARISH" syndrome. Maybe it has something to do with the Law of Supply and Demand (for clergy), but it strikes me that the hierarchy is fearful of asserting its authority in this vital area, and perhaps in other areas as well. Isn't it time you and your brother Cardinals and Bishops assumed command and began applying meaningful controls and performance standards at the parish level? As long as the security of the Sunday collection is left to the naïveté and whims of individual pastors, you won't even be close to attaining that objective.

Finally, Eminence, you'll be pleased to know that, absent any positive expression of interest on your part, this is the last time I will try to reach you directly in this vital matter. If this letter ends up in your "round file" or otherwise fails to impress you with the need for a mandated, diocese-wide collection security system, I will (reluctantly) conclude you're simply out of my direct reach. No matter what, you have my best wishes for success in the many challenges confronting you in today's Church.

Most Sincerely,

Michael W. Ryan

While I ended my letter to Cardinal Law stating it was the last time I would communicate with him on the matter of collection security, I reneged less than a year later and wrote to him on four separate occasions between 1993 and 1997. Cardinal Law did not personally reply to the above letter, but I did receive a reply from then Moderator of the Curia, Bishop Alfred C. Hughes, who said, in pertinent part:

With regard to offertory collections you indicate that you are still working to compel action on this problem. We also continue to work on the alleged infractions. His Eminence has consulted with his Presbyteral Council, we have called together the Pastors Advisory Committee to the Chancellor, we have met with the Regional Bishops and twenty-two vicars of the Archdiocese, we have assembled Regional meetings of Pastors and Finance

Council members and continually bring this matter before groups of new pastors with recent assignments.

With all due respect to Bishop Hughes and that impressive sounding list of actions, the one thing that needed to be done – the implementation of genuinely secure Sunday collection procedures – remained conspicuously undone. Consequently, I felt obliged to reply. Not counting his closing reference to the Almighty, Bishop Hughes acknowledged receipt of my wide-ranging, three-page letter (p.117) with a one-paragraph reply as follows:

> I am sorry that the policies we have put in place and the efforts that we have made do not seem to respond to your expectations. It seems to me that I need to acknowledge that it is not going to be possible to satisfy all your concerns in the way in which you would like them addressed.

Note the complete lack of any reference to the subject of my letter. In this case, it is particularly striking when viewed in light of the fourth paragraph of my letter to him which reads as follows:

> I've also noted an interesting characteristic that seems to run through virtually all of the correspondence I have ever received from Church officials. It is an almost complete avoidance of any specific language that would identify the precise nature of the topic(s) raised in my correspondence. For example, I have made numerous references to theft and embezzlement in prior letters and have even furnished news transcripts dealing with the same terms, but they have been meticulously avoided in all replies.

In February of 1994, I directed a letter (p.121) to Archbishop Daniel W. Kucera, O.S.B., then Chairman of the NCCB Committee on Budget and Finance. In that quite lengthy letter, I cited several specific embezzlement cases, the Church's lack of genuinely secure procedures, and the remarkable turnaround achieved by the parish mentioned in my letter to Cardinal Law. I urged him to use his role as chair of the Budget and Finance Committee to bring the Church into the 20th Century (security-wise) before the rest of the world enters the 21st Century.

Archbishop Kucera replied within two weeks, advising, "I completed my term as chairman of that committee last November. Currently, Archbishop Thomas Murphy of Seattle is the chair. I am forwarding your letter to our NCCB/USCC offices in Washington,

D.C." Needless to say, I was sorry to learn I had corresponded with the wrong prelate, but also pleased that he forwarded my letter to his successor, Archbishop Murphy.

While I had no expectation that Archbishop Murphy would contact me, I waited two months before writing to him in May of 1994. In my letter (p.125), I mentioned Archbishop Kucera's referral and the Pope's impending convocation to consider how the Church can best prepare itself for the Third Millennium. I suggested there is no better way for the Budget and Finance Committee to help prepare the Church for the Third Millennium than to insure the safety and integrity of the Church's main source of income. Archbishop Murphy did not reply.

On November 3, 1994, I directed a letter (p.127) to then NCCB President William Cardinal Keeler, the second of eight NCCB (now USCCB) presidents with whom I have corresponded at least once. While my letters varied in terms of their content and emphasis, I strove to make each letter as clear and complete as possible in order to convey the critical nature of the security issue as well as the urgent need for conference-wide remedial action. In this case, I drew a parallel between the hierarchy's failure to respond to the clergy abuse scourge in a concerted and effective manner, and its failure to recognize and act upon the Sunday collection security issue. I included several case histories and concluded by declaring my readiness to assist, but also noting the "ball" was in his court. Cardinal Keeler did not reply.

Just ten days after my letter to Cardinal Keeler, I penned a follow-up letter (p.130) to NCCB Budget and Finance Committee Chairman Archbishop Murphy. In that letter, I cited correspondence I had with him in 1992 when he chaired the NCCB Committee on Stewardship. I also mentioned the Diocesan Fiscal Management Conference's unresponsiveness in spite of the fact he specifically referred me to them. I concluded by offering to assist in achieving the goal of a genuinely secure collection system. Archbishop Murphy did not reply to my letter, and it would be nearly four months before I made my final attempt to connect with him.

My final letter (p.133) to Archbishop Murphy was written on March 9, 1995. It is particularly noteworthy in that it is the first time I cited the standards of the American Institute of Certified Public Accountants (AICPA), *the* premier authority on accounting standards in the United States. It is also noteworthy in that I suggested the NCCB undertake a definitive test within a designated diocese or archdiocese, using my Sunday collection guidelines to resolve our obvious difference of opinion regarding the integrity of the Church's Sunday collection system. Once again, Archbishop Murphy did not reply.

Two weeks following my letter to Archbishop Murphy, I made my second and final attempt (p.137) to connect with Cardinal Keeler. I included a copy of my letter to Archbishop Murphy, and cited four bible verses I believe have a direct bearing on the hierarchy's failure to secure the collections. I also stressed what it takes to create a genuinely secure environment, and noted how far the Church is from reaching that objective. In retrospect, I threw everything but the proverbial *kitchen sink* at him, including (for the first time) the term *nonfeasance*. I was rewarded with a reply from an Associate General Secretary who merely regurgitated what had become the party line: "The security of the Sunday collections is a matter within the jurisdiction of each diocese." He suggested I might wish to contact the Executive Director of the Diocesan Fiscal Management Conference. Since I had corresponded with that individual and a member of his staff on three previous occasions without receiving even the courtesy of an acknowledgment, I passed on the pleasure of being ignored a fourth time.

On January 1, 1996, I directed a letter (p.140) to the newly elected NCCB President, Bishop Anthony M. Pilla, third of the eight Conference presidents I would write. I made reference to my past efforts to reach his predecessors on the matter of Sunday collection security, and I cited specific embezzlement cases that support the need for action. As I often did, I ended my letter with an offer of assistance, the objective of which I said was "to ensure that our Church does not enter the 21st Century still clinging to woefully deficient, economically debilitating, sin-proliferating, 19th Century methods and procedures."

Like the response to my last letter to Cardinal Keeler, my letter to Bishop Pilla was also answered by a staffer, this time an Associate General Secretary who stated that the Accounting Practices Committee recognized "the incidence and severity of fraud in the Church over the past few years" and "has recently completed a manual entitled *Diocesan Internal Controls, A Framework.*" He concluded by stating that I should "be assured that the bishops have recognized and are addressing this problem."

With a great deal of suspicion, and before replying to the Associate General Secretary, I purchased and reviewed a copy of *Diocesan*

Internal Controls, A Framework.[44] My suspicion was not unwarranted. To begin with, the manual was not written for parish use but rather for diocesan fiscal managers. As a result, its coverage of the Sunday collection consists of one very short paragraph entitled "Handling of Collections" that contains so little guidance it is virtually useless. Indeed, some of what little was said could well help to mask and perpetuate ongoing thefts. In marked contrast to the paucity of information on collection security, other financial elements (receivables, disbursements, payroll, etc.) were covered in considerable detail.

As the Sunday collection is the Church's primary source of income and, by its very nature, the most vulnerable to repetitive surreptitious theft, the exclusion of secure procedures from that manual, coupled with the NCCB's failure to publish them in any other manual for parishes, confirms (at least in my mind) their nonfeasance.

In light of the Associate General Secretary's unsatisfactory response, I replied to him in March of 1996, pointing out the manual's lack of any meaningful guidelines on how to secure the collections. At the same time, I wrote a second letter (p.143) to Bishop Pilla, enclosing a copy of my reply to the Associate General Secretary and urging Bishop Pilla to promote the conference-wide implementation of secure procedures to both deter and detect embezzlements from the Sunday collections. Again, I assured him of my availability and willingness to help the NCCB ensure that the Catholic Church does not "enter the 21th Century still clinging to grossly deficient 19th Century procedures." Neither Bishop Pilla nor the Associate General Secretary replied.

In August of 1996, I sent a follow-up letter to the same Associate General Secretary. I noted his failure to reply to my prior letter and shared with him a syllogism that had come to mind as I was pondering the hierarchy's knowing and willful failure to secure the collections. That syllogism reads as follows:

> Major Premise: The <u>proximate</u> cause of all Sunday collection embezzlements is the moral weakness of the individuals who commit such embezzlements.

> Minor Premise: Elementary yet effective security measures the hierarchy is well aware of but consciously refuses to implement would prevent most Sunday collection embezzlements.

> Conclusion: The <u>ultimate</u> cause of most Sunday collection embezzlements is the hierarchy's conscious refusal to implement effective security measures.

The Associate General Secretary did not reply. On January 22, 1997, I sent a third letter (p.144) to Bishop Pilla and included a copy of my letter to the Associate General Secretary. Having given further thought to the syllogism I had sent to the Associate General Secretary, I took it to the next level and incorporated that into my letter to Bishop Pilla. That syllogism reads as follows:

> Major Premise: Embezzlement [the unauthorized, surreptitious removal/misappropriation of funds] from the Sunday collection - whether committed by a pastor, priest, employee or volunteer - is a sin.

> Minor Premise: <u>Most</u> Sunday collection embezzlements <u>and their concomitant sins</u> can be prevented by simple, inexpensive security measures the U. S. Catholic hierarchy is well aware of but refuses to employ.

> Conclusion: The U. S. Catholic hierarchy bears <u>ultimate</u> responsibility for the sins that flow from <u>most</u> Sunday collection embezzlements.

I asked Bishop Pilla to review the two syllogisms and advise whether they are correct and, if incorrect, to advise me of the particulars. I noted that if the syllogisms are correct, he and his fellow prelates have a crucial decision to make: continue to be the ultimate cause of most Sunday collection thefts and the sins they represent, or swallow their pride and do what clearly needs to be done. I ended my letter with this quote from Luke (17:1):

> Things that make people fall into sin are bound to happen, but how terrible for the one who makes them happen!

That letter elicited the following response from Bishop Pilla. It is one of only a handful letters I elected to keep in the body of this chapter because of its significance. In this case, Bishop Pilla's letter is significant for what it does not contain, and that is any reference to the two syllogisms.

Office of the President
3211 Fourth Street NE
Washington DC 20017-1194
(202) 541-3100 FAX (202) 541-3166

Most Reverend Anthony M. Pilla, D.D., M.A.
Bishop of Cleveland
President

January 31, 1997

Dear Mr. Ryan:

I write in response to your letter of January 22, 1997 regarding security for Sunday collection funds.

As Msgr. [name withheld] wrote to you in January of 1996, the Accounting Practices Committee of the United States Catholic Conference has discussed the matter and has proposed means for bishops to develop better internal financial controls at the diocesan level. As you may know, the Conference cannot legislate directives for all bishops to follow, but does provide information to assist bishops in their administrative responsibilities. Although I am certain that the Church is not immune from the evil of fraud and embezzlement, I am confident that the bishops of this country are aware of this issue and that they take appropriate measures in their dioceses to safeguard against it.

With gratitude for your concern, I am

Sincerely yours in Christ,

Most Reverend Anthony M. Pilla

Bishop of Cleveland
President

Because I viewed Bishop Pilla's response as being wholly inadequate, I wrote a fourth letter (p.147) to him on March 4, 1997. I pointed out the lack of any meaningful measures to protect the Church's primary source of income, and both his and his predecessors' failure to acknowledge or attempt to refute the negative moral ramifications of their "ongoing failure to curtail the perennial evil of Sunday collection theft." Bishop Pilla did not reply.

More than two and a half years later, I put my oar in the water with Bishop Pilla's successor and the fourth Conference president I would write, Bishop Joseph A. Fiorenza. In that letter (p.149), I outlined my past efforts and pointed out the inadequacy of existing guidelines to protect the collections. I also cited several embezzlement cases and enclosed a brochure I noted contained far more detail on how collection funds must be protected than do all twenty-two pages of their much vaunted Publication #5-056, *Diocesan Internal Controls, A Framework*. I ended the letter expressing my willingness to assist the NCCB "in any way possible."

An Associate General Secretary, a CPA with "extensive experience in dealing with the issues" I raised, responded to my letter to Bishop Fiorenza on December 7, 1999. His response (p.152) is important because it introduced Canon Law for the first time in my then ten-year quest for reform. In effect, he stated that Canon Law prohibits the Conference from issuing instructions on how Sunday collection funds must be handled within individual dioceses. Needless to say, this caused me to research Canon Law where I zeroed in on two canons, one of which turned out not to apply. The other, Canon 455, proved to be dead on target as will be explained in greater depth toward the end of this chapter.

I replied to the Associate General Secretary on December 12, 1999 (p.154), pointing out the two canons, but he did not reply. While I had mailed a copy of that letter to Bishop Fiorenza, the tenor of the Associate General Secretary's letter conveyed the impression President Fiorenza had not even seen my letter of November 28, 1999. Consequently, I directed a follow-up letter (p.157) to Bishop Fiorenza at his home diocese in Houston on December 29, 1999. I enclosed a copy of my prior letter and informed him that my collection security guidelines were then (and remain to this day) available for download at no cost from my own website. As before, I expressed my readiness to assist.

Having received no reply from Bishop Fiorenza, I wrote to him a third time in March of 2000. In that letter (p.159), I advised him that I was in the process of preparing a petition to the Holy See, and I was wondering if he wished to be characterized as "the third NCCB President who chose to stand mute and allow the thoroughly discredited response of a subordinate to represent his position on the topics of revenue protection, embezzlement and unnecessary temptation within the U.S. Catholic Church."

While Bishop Fiorenza did not reply, the same NCCB Associate General Secretary who replied to my letter of November 28, 1999 also replied to this letter on March 27, 2000. He acknowledged receipt of the letter to Bishop Fiorenza and stated that he (the AGS) would be meeting with a group of bishops in April "to discuss accountability and the canons which are applicable." I took that as an invitation to reply, and I did so on April 4, 2000. In that letter (p.161), I suggested the bishops include in their discussions certain scripture readings as well as the AICPA standards I had referred to Archbishop Murphy in 1995. I also asked to be informed of the outcome of his meeting. No reply was received, thus prompting a follow-up letter (p.165) in mid-June.

In that letter, I reminded the Associate General Secretary that I was in the process of preparing a detailed petition to the Holy See, and that I wanted to be sure to convey the NCCB's current position and rationale as accurately as possible. He replied on June 20 and, in so many words, advised me that the bishops' deliberations are confidential and, further, cautioned me that any petition to the Holy See should not contain any speculation about "what the Conference may be thinking, doing or saying" in regard to the matter of Sunday collection security. Reading between the lines, his response had a *we'll come after you if you say anything derogatory* tone to it.

Implied threats notwithstanding, I sent a packet to the Vatican on February 14, 2001. It consisted of a cover letter and a four-page petition accompanied by over one hundred pages of exhibits. I mailed it to the Vatican in the person of His Eminence Joseph Cardinal Ratzinger, then Prefect of the Congregation for the Doctrine of the Faith. The cover letter and petition follow. Aside from the fact that the petition was addressed to the cardinal who now heads the Catholic Church as Pope Benedict XVI, the petition is noteworthy by virtue of what it contained in comparison to the reply it elicited.

[letterhead]

February 14, 2001

His Eminence Joseph Cardinal Ratzinger
Sacred Congregation for the Doctrine of Faith
Piazza del S. Uffizio 11
00193 Rome, Italy

Your Eminence:

The accompanying document entitled *Petition for Examination and Resolution* is being presented to you under provisions of Canon Law (Book II, Part I, Title I, Canon 212 §3) which concern the obligations and rights of Christ's Faithful. A copy of my résumé is attached to establish that I do possess the "*knowledge, competence and position*" required of those who desire or feel obliged "*to manifest to the sacred Pastors their views on matters which concern the good of the Church.*"

   With due respect, this is not an attempt to bypass my own bishop or the U. S. Catholic Hierarchy. Rather, as I believe you will come to recognize, it is a last resort, a final plea in my ten-year effort to make one crucial point: the Church's primary source of revenue, the Sunday collection, is highly vulnerable to repetitive, surreptitious, internal theft, a serious sin which often leads to or facilitates other serious sins. In light of that fact, I believe morality and common sense demand that the Sunday collection be afforded an appropriate and uniform level of protection.

   Over the past ten years, Your Eminence, I have corresponded with Cardinal Law and various members of his staff, and with four Presidents of the Conference of Catholic Bishops as well as many other USCCB officials. Without exception, and notwithstanding the morally and fiscally deleterious effects directly attributable to the status quo, all of my pleas for corrective measures have fallen upon seemingly deaf ears. I am confident the accompanying documents will clearly establish that the United States hierarchy refuses to even acknowledge a problem exists, let alone take action to correct it.

   It is my firm belief, one which I hope you will conclude is fully supported by the accompanying petition, that the issue of revenue protection contains strong spiritual and theological elements in addition to the obvious fiduciary and administrative aspects. For that reason, and based upon the assumption that spiritual matters take primacy over temporal matters, I concluded that you, Your Eminence, are the proper recipient. However, if my assumption is incorrect, I would appreciate being so informed in connection with your referral of the file to the correct office of the Holy See.

Most sincerely,

Michael W. Ryan

THE VATICAN PETITION

Petition for Examination and Resolution
of the interrelated matters of repetitive, surreptitious theft, and the sins
and occasions of sin generated and countenanced by an intentionally
vulnerable revenue handling process

The phenomenon of covert theft or embezzlement from the community purse can be traced back to the Twelve Apostles, and can be reasonably and logically assumed to have been a recurring phenomenon from Jesus' time to the present day. As JOHN [12:6] chronicled, "*He carried the money bag and would help himself from it.*"

This petition proposes to establish that, at least throughout the United States, Sunday collection funds, the Church's primary source of revenue, remain highly vulnerable to surreptitious theft and are thereby a leading cause of temptation to sin and actual sin within the Church. It is further postulated that the extreme vulnerability of those funds is directly attributable to the hierarchy's knowing and willful refusal to consider readily-available, low-cost security measures that would all but eliminate not only the incidence of such thefts but also the temptation that leads to the sin of theft. The petitioner holds that the remedy requires uniform, Church-wide security measures.

The petitioner believes that his hypothesis and recommendations are supported by Holy Scripture, Canon Law and certain professional standards relating to the obligation of managers to protect income and assets. Each of those references is identified and summarized as follows:

Holy Scripture

LUKE 17:1 [Matthew 18:7] - *"Things that make people fall into sin are bound to happen, but how terrible for the one who makes them happen."*

LUKE 12:2 [MATTHEW 10:26] - *"Whatever is covered up will be uncovered, and every secret will be made known."*

Code of Canon Law

Book V, Title I, Canon 1265 §2: *The Episcopal Conference can draw up rules regarding collections, which must be observed by all. . . .*

Book V, Title II, Canon 1284, §1 and § 2: *All administrators are to perform their duties with the diligence of a good householder. Therefore they must: 1° be vigilant that no goods placed in their care in any way perish or suffer damage;*

Statement on Auditing Standards, Codification of Auditing Standards and Procedures, issued by the American Institute of Certified Public Accountants in 1973. Pertinent sections as follows:

Section 110.02: *Management has the responsibility for adopting sound accounting policies, for maintaining an adequate and effective system of accounts, for safeguarding assets, and for devising a system of internal control that will, among other things, help assure the production of proper financial statements.*

Section 320.42: *The objective of safeguarding assets requires that access be limited to authorized personnel. The number and caliber of personnel to whom access is authorized should be influenced by the nature of the assets and the related susceptibility to loss through errors and irregularities. Limitation of direct access to assets requires appropriate physical segregation and protective equipment or devices.*

Section 320.44: *. . . agreement of a cash count with the recorded balance does not provide evidence that all cash received has been properly recorded. This illustrates an unavoidable distinction between fiduciary and recorded accountability: the former arises immediately upon acquisition of an asset; the latter arises only when the initial record of the transaction is prepared.*

Section 320.67: *Controls and weaknesses affecting different classes of transactions are not offsetting in their effect. For example, weaknesses in cash receipts procedures are not mitigated by controls in cash disbursements procedures;*

Section 320.68: *The auditor's evaluation of accounting control with reference to each significant class of transactions and related assets should be a conclusion as to whether the prescribed procedures and compliance therewith are satisfactory . . . The procedures and compliance should be considered satisfactory if the auditor's review and tests disclose no condition he believes to be a material weakness . . . [i.e.] . . . a condition in which the auditor believes the prescribed procedures or the degree of compliance with them does not provide reasonable assurance that errors or irregularities in amounts that would be material in financial statements being audited would be prevented or detected within a timely period by employees in the normal course of performing their assigned functions.*

Diocesan Internal Controls: A Framework (issued by Committee on Budget & Finance, National Conference of Catholic Bishops/United States Catholic Conference in 1995)

Handling of Collections [The named document's only reference to Sunday collection procedures]

[Author's note: As the paragraph that appeared in the Vatican petition is copyrighted, it has been excised from this work.]

Procedure to Assist Pastors in the Internal Control of Finances (issued by the Archdiocese of Boston in 1992) A copy of this document is included in the supporting papers.

Present Conditions

Insofar as present-day conditions are concerned, this petition includes current examples of major intra-organizational embezzlements which establish that the referenced phenomenon has not only carried forward but has exacted a heavy moral toll in addition to its debilitating economic effects. And when one considers that Judas constituted a significant percentage of the Church's then total membership, the weekly availability of large sums of uncounted, unsecured currency to literally thousands of individuals in the United States alone is disconcerting, to say the least.

The Issue

Two basic questions lie at the root of this matter. First, to what extent is the hierarchy morally obliged to provide an adequate level of protection for cash offerings made by Christ's Faithful and, second, to what extent is the hierarchy morally obliged to eliminate proven occasions of sin which exist within the realm of their authority and responsibility?

Insofar as the first question is concerned, there are at least two good reasons to conclude that the hierarchy is obliged to provide an adequate level of protection. The first reason is rather obvious: Christ's Faithful give in the belief that their offerings will be used to further the work of His Church. Consequently, they have a right to expect that what they place in the collection is, in fact, properly deposited in the bank. But under the timeworn procedures now used in virtually every parish, no one can <u>confirm</u> that significant losses are not occurring each and every week of the year. In essence, this state of uncertainty constitutes a failure to ensure that goods placed in the Church's care do not in any way perish or suffer damage. And the fact that, at the Conference level, this failure is both knowing and willful would appear to compound its seriousness.

The 2nd reason for providing an adequate level of protection is seldom considered but also concerns individual rights: the right of employees and volunteers <u>not</u> involved in the collection to be free of suspicion in the event of an unexplained loss. When security over a church's Sunday collection is absent or weak and a loss occurs, <u>every person</u> having access to the areas where those funds are stored and/or processed <u>must</u> be deemed suspect. This viewpoint is axiomatic of sound criminal investigative and law enforcement practices.

The second question, regarding the extent to which the hierarchy is morally obliged to eliminate proven occasions of sin which exist within the realm of their authority and responsibility, is a theological matter and, as such, is outside the realm of the petitioner's expertise. With a view toward assisting the Holy See in resolving that question as it relates to the subject of this petition, however, transcripts of newspaper articles relating to several embezzlement cases are presented as additional exhibits. In most instances, the reviewer will note that the sin of theft either led to or abetted other sins separate and apart from the theft. The petitioner maintains that, in many if not most instances, the thief's concomitant sins would not have been committed if he or she had been denied the opportunity to commit the sin of theft.

Insofar as the hierarchy's ability to eliminate or at least drastically reduce the opportunity for and incidence of theft from the Sunday collection, it remains for the petitioner to explain how that goal can be achieved with minimal expense and effort. This is not to imply that financial factors should in any way control a moral imperative, but rather to demonstrate that the costs are truly minimal, especially when contrasted with the great moral good they will generate. In that regard, however, it is important to note that decades of neglect have created certain entrenched attitudes at the parish level; in the petitioner's opinion, those attitudes can only be overcome by forthright, authoritative directives which leave no doubt as to who is in charge and what must be done.

Before the level of security over any Sunday collection system can be considered adequate, the following general criteria must be met. First, the collection for each Mass or service must be positively secured, immediately after it is taken up. The method used must be such that each person in the chain of custody (from church vestibule to counting room and all points between) will know, through simple visual inspection, whether anyone had or could have had access to the funds. Second, detailed, written operating procedures must be developed for the collection, interim storage and counting operations. The counting procedures must provide for the presence of at least three counters and establish unbroken observation and control over the funds (especially the currency) by at least two (2) persons, from the moment the storage containers are opened until all funds have been counted independently by two (2) persons, verified, recorded on a witnessed bank deposit slip, and locked/sealed in a bank deposit bag. And third, each week's count must be documented via standardized forms designed so that, when completed, they clearly reflect whether or not the required counting and verification procedures were followed.

The petitioner's personal experience has shown that the average parish can implement secure collection procedures for not more than three hundred dollars U.S. Further, that figure could be significantly reduced if bulk purchases were made at the diocesan level. When one considers the previously mentioned newspaper articles, it can be seen that the cost of implementing these procedures would, in some instances, be recovered by less than one week's savings in collection funds that would otherwise have disappeared due to theft. Again, however, the petitioner is not in any way attempting to equate or establish a conditional relationship between the cost of the program and the moral imperative to eliminate what is virtually a Church-wide occasion of sin.

Finally, the petitioner respectfully calls attention to the fact that detailed collection security guidelines are now and have been available at no charge whatsoever. These guidelines contain complete details on how to secure a Sunday collection, including a description of the low-cost equipment required to accomplish that objective. The guidelines have been furnished to the U. S. Conference on more than one occasion over the past ten years and may be downloaded from the Internet at http://www.gis.net/~pss. A copy of those guidelines, which now include guidelines for protecting a church's disbursements operations, is appended to the accompanying exhibits. The petitioner will be pleased to answer, to the best of his ability, any questions that may arise in connection with the Holy See's examination, and to provide any additional documentation that might be needed to ensure that the examination can be conducted without undue impediment.

Based upon the petitioner's experience to date, and with all due respect for the expertise, opinions and priorities of the U. S. Conference, any decision to refer this petition to the U. S. Conference without examination, deliberation and preliminary findings by the Holy See will be tantamount to disposing of the petition as meaningless nuisance correspondence. The accompanying documents clearly establish that the U. S. Conference, for reasons best known to its leaders, has no interest in creating a truly secure Sunday collection system, and is even willing to abide the recurring sin of preventable theft to ensure that the status quo is preserved.

Respectfully submitted,

Michael W. Ryan

The exhibits included copies of most if not all of the previously described correspondence as well as the particulars of seventeen embezzlements, twelve of which involved members of the clergy. Much to my disappointment, the file was referred to another congregation. In a four-sentence reply dated March 30, 2001, Archbishop Csaba Ternyak, Secretary of the Congregation for the Clergy, merely regurgitated the NCCB's mantra. Following is his reply.

CONGREGATIO
PRO CLERICIS
———

Vatican City, 30 March, 2001

Prot. N. 20010612

Mr. Michael W. Ryan

   Thank you for your letter dated 14th February 2001, which was kindly forwarded, to this Congregation, competent for issues of administration, by the Congregation for the Doctrine of the Faith.

   The issue that you raise concerning the security of the 'Sunday collection' is something that would fall under the competency of the local Bishop. This Dicastery notes that you have made your views known to a number of Ordinaries and the Conference of Catholic Bishops, and now, as such, it is left to their prudent judgment as to whether they accept and adopt your proposals.

   I take this opportunity to renew my sentiments of esteem and with every best wish, I remain,

Yours sincerely in Christ,

+ *Csaba Ternyák*
Secr.

   As the reader will note, the Vatican did nothing more than rubber stamp the NCCB's already thoroughly discredited position. I expressed my disappointment in a follow-up letter (p.167), only to receive a response advising that the Congregation for the Clergy "has nothing more to add to its response already given in our letter dated 30th March, 2001, Protocol Number 20010612."

   Having been politely put off by the Vatican, I turned back to the USCCB in the person of its newly elected President, Bishop Wilton D. Gregory, the fifth president with whom I would correspond. I included with my letter (p.170) a copy of my petition to the Holy See, and I expressed my disappointment in the Holy See's refusal to do anything more that rubber stamp what I termed "the U.S. Conference's thoroughly disproved stance."

I was pleased to receive a reply (p.172) from Bishop Gregory within three weeks of my letter to him. He is the first USCCB president who appeared to do more than ignore or dismiss my request out of hand. Based upon a briefing he received from the Conference staff, however, Bishop Gregory delivered the party line: "we are not empowered either canonically or by our Conference statutes and bylaws to address the question of internal controls over offertory collections in such a way as to standardize or require any particular procedures."

The real issue, of course, is not whether the Conference is empowered to require any particular procedures, but rather whether it can become so empowered. And the answer to that is a resounding YES! Canon 455 (included in Chapter V in its entirety) clearly provides the means by which the USCCB can issue general decrees affecting all dioceses within the U.S. Conference.

In regard to Canon 455, and as noted toward the end of Chapter V, the USCCB's website lists twenty-nine "complementary norms" approved by the USCCB for Conference-wide application since the revised Code of Canon Law was promulgated in 1983. A number of those norms required *and* received Vatican approval under provisions of Canon 455 as evidenced by the following statement posted at the Conference's website: "Those actions requiring *recognitio* or approval from the Apostolic See in accord with canon 455§2 have been reviewed by the appropriate Roman dicastery."[45]

In his reply, Bishop Gregory stated, "I am also mindful of the autonomy of the diocesan Bishop and what can and cannot be legislated or required from the national level." As "autonomy" is a recurring element of the Conference's refusal to act at the national level, it is appropriate to examine the meaning of that word. Merriam-Webster defines *autonomy* as follows:

1: the quality or state of being self-governing; *especially*: the right of self-government

2: self-directing freedom and especially moral independence

3: a self-governing state[46]

Based upon their inaction in the matter of Sunday collection security, one can only assume the bishops place a higher value on their secular authority (autonomy) than they do on the wellbeing of the Church's principal source of revenue, not to mention the moral wellbeing of those who succumb each week to the temptation presented by highly vulnerable Sunday collections.

In a wide-ranging follow-up letter (p.174) to Bishop Gregory, I noted the Conference had engaged in more than a decade of dissembling and obfuscation to ensure that hundreds (probably thousands) of Sunday collection thieves can continue their thievery unfettered. Bishop Gregory did not reply, however, thereby giving rise to a third letter (p.177) in which I drew a parallel between the sexual abuse scandal, Sunday collection thefts and the hierarchy's refusal to implement secure procedures. I also linked their nonfeasance to sins of omission, asking him whether the Conference's knowing failure to eradicate a specific temptation to sin, one which is well within their power to eradicate, would constitute a sin of omission.

Once again, Bishop Gregory did not reply, thus giving rise to a fourth and final letter (p.180) in January of 2004. In this letter, and having no doubt about the Conference's access to the empowering provisions of Canon 455, I challenged Bishop Gregory's assertion that the Conference is "not empowered either canonically or by our Conference statutes and bylaws to address the question of internal controls over offertory collections in such a way as to standardize or require any particular procedures." I asked him whether there is a procedure by which the Conference could become empowered, and I then cited Canon 455.

Bishop Gregory never replied to the above letter. However, I mentioned three items in that letter that warrant elaboration. The first is a reference to #2287 in the Catholic Catechism. That section reads as follows:

> Anyone who uses the power at his disposal in such a way that it leads others to do wrong becomes guilty of scandal and responsible for the evil that he has directly or indirectly encouraged. 'Temptations to sin are sure to come; but woe to him by whom they come!'[47]

The quote within #2287 is the words of Jesus as recorded in Luke 17:1. The point I was making, of course, is that the USCCB's knowing failure to mandate genuinely secure Sunday collection procedures conference-wide has perpetuated a temptation to sin that would not otherwise exist.

The second item is my reference to the resignation of former Oklahoma Governor Frank A. Keating as head of the National Review Board. Created by the USCCB in 2002, the Board's mission was to monitor implementation of the USCCB's "Charter for the Protection of Children and Young People"[48] in the wake of the clerical abuse scandal. In his letter of resignation to then USCCB President Gregory, Governor Keating said, in pertinent part:

> Our Church is a Faith institution, a home to Christ's people. It is not a criminal enterprise. It does not condone and cover up criminal activity. It does not follow a code of silence. My remarks, which some bishops found offensive, were deadly accurate. I make no apology. To resist grand jury subpoenas, to suppress the names of offending clerics, to deny, to obfuscate, to explain away; that is the model of a criminal organization, not my church.[49]

According to news reports at the time, Governor Keating was incensed by the resistance of one or more unnamed prelates to the Board's investigations.

The third item was a newspaper article I enclosed with my letter. The article detailed the case of a priest who, in connection with a police investigation into harassing telephone calls, was found to be in possession of an unlicensed gun, pornographic magazines and videos, photos of Hitler, Nazi memorabilia and $88,000 in cash, some still contained in envelopes from the prior Sunday's collection. When police asked him about the money, he reportedly replied, "That's my 401(k) Plan."[50] My purpose in providing Bishop Gregory that article was to point out that the priest was aided in his errant proclivities by his apparently unfettered access to Sunday collections.

My next approach was to Bishop William S. Skylstad, Bishop Gregory's successor and, for those who are keeping score, the sixth Conference president I would approach. In retrospect, it seems I was not in the best frame of mind when I wrote the letter (p.183) but it is a matter of record and I believe it is not without merit. As a matter of fact, and while Bishop Skylstad never responded, it's entirely possible something I said in that letter helped trigger activities that culminated in the issuance of a document by the USCCB Treasurer a little more than one year later. Included in my letter to Bishop Skylstad was this statement:

I have had two articles published in the Catholic periodical *New Oxford Review*, and I am presently working on a third article which will draw upon the themes of the first two and, in effect, clearly and firmly establish responsibility for the lack of secure procedures squarely in the lap of the USCCB.

In addition, I named the two articles I had written, the first of which is entitled "The Second Greatest Scandal in the Church."

On March 23, 2007, USCCB Treasurer Bishop Dennis M. Schnurr issued a four-page document consisting of a one-page memorandum addressed to "All Bishops" under the subject "Parish Financial Governance," and a three-page attachment entitled "USCCB Accounting Practices Committee Recommendations." In his transmittal, Bishop Schnurr stated, "some in the media and elsewhere have coined Church finances as the next big scandal for the Catholic Church."

Aside from conveying the impression the USCCB was beginning to *hear footsteps* and see traces of *handwriting on the wall*, the communications are of particular interest because of what they *do not* address in any substantive way: the Church's principal source of income, the Sunday collection. The memorandum and attachment follow.

Finance Office
3211 Fourth Street, NE
Washington, DC 20017-1194
202-541-3028 FAX 202-722-8728

MEMORANDUM

TO: All Bishops

FROM: Most Reverend Dennis M. Schnurr, Treasurer

DATE: March 23, 2007

RE: Parish Financial Governance

As we are all painfully aware, the Church is not immune to financial malfeasance, a fact that has become increasingly clear in recent months as financial scandals have been reported from all over the country. In fact, some in the media and elsewhere have coined Church finances as the next big scandal for the Catholic Church. A number of articles have appeared as of late on this topic in various newspapers such as the *Wall Street Journal, New York Times, USA Today* and *Time Magazine*. In today's environment of the Enrons, Worldcoms, et al, the Church must remain vigilant. It must continuously seek measures and procedures that can better ensure that the monies and resources are being expended in accordance with the intention of donors and benefactors. A sampling of recent media stories follow:

In New Jersey, a priest was sentenced in June 2006 to five years in prison after the misappropriation of $2 million.

In Ohio, the CFO was charged in August 2006 with participating in a kickback scheme totaling nearly $785,000. The CFO had left one diocese and was working as the Director of Finance for another diocese when the 23 count federal indictment related to the first diocese was handed down.

In Florida, two priests were charged in September 2006 with skimming more than $8.6 million from a parish.

In Illinois, a priest was indicted in October 2006 on charges of stealing more than $190,000 from a parish.

In New York, four church procurement officials allegedly conspired to extort $2 million from vendors who provided food to church schools and parishes.

In December 2006, a survey by researchers at Villanova University found that 85% of dioceses that responded had discovered embezzlement of church money in the last five years, with 11% reporting that more than $500,000 had been stolen. While this report is somewhat misleading in that it seems to imply that 85% of the institutions (i.e., over 19,000 parishes, 8,000 schools, etc.) within the dioceses are experiencing fraud, the report has received national media attention.

In Connecticut, a priest was removed in January 2007 over the disappearance of approximately $500,000. This followed a report late last year in which another priest in Connecticut had embezzled approximately $1.4 million.

In Virginia, a priest has just recently (January 2007) been accused of stealing over $600,000.

At this time, there are ongoing investigations of fraudulent activity in Texas and Pennsylvania.

The USCCB Accounting Practices Committee (APC), composed of 11 CPA/CFO members from the dioceses, four members representing LCWR and CMSM, five CPA advisers from large public accounting firms, and the USCCB CFO serving as staff, has had on its agenda for some time a study of parish financial governance. The vast majority of the aforementioned frauds appear to be occurring at the parish level. At the APC meeting in January 2007, this topic was thoroughly studied and several recommendations were made to enhance the financial governance in the 19,000+ parishes. A summary of the APC recommendations can be found on the following page.

The Committee on Budget and Finance has reviewed the recommendations of the APC and supports them as "best practices." To that end, I recommend that serious consideration be given to the implementation of these best practices in all of our dioceses. The APC will be developing tools, such as a parish reporting form, to assist with the implementation of its recommendations.

I trust and hope this information is helpful to you. If I can be of any assistance, please do not hesitate to contact me.

USCCB ACCOUNTING PRACTICES COMMITTEE RECOMMENDATIONS

The USCCB Accounting Practices Committee (APC) met on January 11-12, 2007 and discussed the financial governance challenges that face the 19,000+ parishes which deal primarily in cash from the collection plate. While the APC has drafted the following recommendations to improve existing diocesan policies relative to financial governance at the parish level, the APC acknowledges that many dioceses already have very good policies in place. Accordingly, the recommendations which follow should be viewed in the context of being enhancements and/or a re-doubling of efforts, where applicable. In addition, the APC affirms that these recommendations must be complimentary to the work being done by the Diocesan Fiscal Management Conference (DFMC) on the internal audits of parishes, under the auspices of the USCCB Ad Hoc Committee on Diocesan Audits.

SHORTER TERM RECOMMENDATIONS

- In the foreword to *Diocesan Internal Controls*, which was created by the APC and published by the USCCB Committee on Budget and Finance in 1995, Archbishop Murphy, then-Treasurer, notes that "Canon 1284 states that all administrators are to perform their duties with the diligence of a good householder. The bishop can delegate the authority but not the responsibility. He has the duty to ensure that no abuses exist in the administration of church goods within the diocese." The executive summary of that document points out, "Although the bishop will not become too involved in the details of the internal control system, he is the only person who has the power to ensure that each area of a diocese carries out its responsibility for the system. The proper tone must be set at the top of the organization, and for a diocese, that is the bishop." The APC again affirms that there must be effective oversight by the bishop for compliance with all diocesan policies in each area of the diocese, and each of the following recommendations made are made within that overarching mindset.

- The APC recognizes the extreme importance of a properly functioning parish finance council as it relates to proper parish governance and internal controls. To that end, and similar to the USCCB resolution entitled *Diocesan Financial Reporting*, the APC recommends that annually each parish send a letter to the diocesan bishop containing:

  o The names and professional titles of the members of the parish finance council

  o The dates on which the parish finance council has met during the preceding fiscal year and since the end of the fiscal year

  o The date(s) on which the approved (i.e.-by the parish finance council) parish financial statements/budgets were made available to the parishioners during the preceding fiscal year and since the end of the fiscal year. A copy of said published financial statements/budgets should be provided to the bishop

  o A statement signed by the parish priest and the finance council members that they have met, developed, and discussed the financial statements and budget of the parish

- The APC recommends that thorough diocesan training be provided to the parish finance council members relative to their roles and responsibilities.

- The APC recommends that diocesan policies exist for conflicts of interest, whistleblower, and fraud (including prosecution in all cases). These policies must be applicable in each area of the diocese.

- The APC recommends that each parish complete an annual internal control questionnaire and that a proper review and follow-up be made by qualified diocesan personnel.

- The APC recognizes that the DFMC is working on a position paper outlining the rationale and importance of internal audits of parishes, which is extremely important to the entire process of the financial governance of parishes.

LONGER TERM RECOMMENDATIONS

- The APC recommends that a parish best practices manual be developed, similar to *Diocesan Financial Issues* which has been developed for the dioceses.

- The APC recommends that financial training be integrated into current seminarian programs (and/or ongoing faith formation programs) such that students will be better prepared to handle these eventualities.

Note that of the six case histories mentioned by Bishop Schnurr, not one is identified as relating to the Church's principal source of revenue, the Sunday collection, and nowhere in his memorandum is the Sunday collection mentioned. Apparently preferring to characterize embezzlements as "frauds," Bishop Schnurr notes:

The vast majority of the aforementioned frauds appear to be occurring at the parish level. At the APC meeting in January 2007, this topic was thoroughly studied and several recommendations were made to enhance the financial governance in the 19,000+ parishes.

Quite stunningly, the USCCB Accounting Practices Committee's "Recommendations" contain only one reference to the Church's primary source of income, and that reference is in the opening sentence which reads as follows:

The USCCB Accounting Practices Committee (APC) met on January 11-12, 2007 and discussed the financial governance challenges that face the 19,000+ parishes which deal primarily in cash from the collection plate. (emphasis added)

So here we have the APC acknowledging - in the very first sentence of their three-page report on the subject of "Parish Financial Governance" - that parishes "deal primarily in cash from the collection plate," but then proceeding to the end of the report without ever again mentioning the Sunday collection. How on earth does any committee begin a report by naming the core issue and then complete the report without making any further reference to that issue? Knowing what I do about the USCCB's mindset, the most logical explanation is that the subject was intentionally omitted. You see, narrative concerning the safety of the Sunday collection would open the door to questions regarding the implementation of secure procedures which, in turn, would open the door to questions about the level from which such procedures should be promulgated - and that is a discussion the USCCB refuses to entertain.

Bishop Schnurr described the makeup of the Accounting Practices Committee as consisting of "11 CPA/CFO members from the dioceses, four members representing LCWR and CMSM, five CPA advisers from large public accounting firms, and the USCCB CFO." The acronyms LCWR and CMSM stand for the *Leadership Conference of Women Religious* and the *Conference of Major Superiors of Men*, respectively. With a blue-ribbon committee such as that described by Bishop Schnurr, one can only marvel at how they completely missed the target.

If not directed toward the issue the APC was ostensibly tasked to address, i.e., "the financial governance challenges that face the 19,000+ parishes which deal primarily in cash from the collection plate," what did that blue-ribbon group focus their attention upon? The short answer is *appearances* which can best be appreciated by reviewing, in pertinent part, the APC recommendations a second time, this time with emphasis added.

- The APC recognizes the extreme importance of a properly functioning parish finance council as it relates to proper parish governance and internal controls. To that end, and similar to the USCCB resolution entitled Diocesan Financial Reporting, the APC recommends that annually <u>each parish send a letter to the diocesan bishop</u> containing:

  o The <u>names and professional titles of the members of the parish finance council</u>

  o The <u>dates on which the parish finance council has met</u> during the preceding fiscal year and since the end of the fiscal year

  o The <u>date(s) on which the approved (i.e.-by the parish finance council) parish financial statements/budgets were made available to the parishioners</u> during the preceding fiscal year and since the end of the fiscal year. A copy of said published financial statements/budgets should be provided to the bishop.

  o <u>A statement signed by the parish priest and the finance council members that they have met, developed, and</u>

discussed the financial statements and budget of the parish

- The APC recommends that thorough diocesan training be provided to the parish finance council members relative to their roles and responsibilities.

- The APC recommends that diocesan policies exist for conflicts of interest, whistleblower, and fraud (including prosecution in all cases). These policies must be applicable in each area of the diocese.

- The APC recommends that each parish complete an annual internal control questionnaire and that a proper review and follow-up be made by qualified diocesan personnel.

- The APC recognizes that the DFMC is working on a position paper outlining the rationale and importance of internal audits of parishes, which is extremely important to the entire process of the financial governance of parishes.

LONGER TERM RECOMMENDATIONS

- The APC recommends that a parish best practices manual be developed, similar to Diocesan Financial Issues which has been developed for the dioceses.

- The APC recommends that financial training be integrated into current seminarian programs (and/or ongoing faith formation programs) such that students will be better prepared to handle these eventualities. (emphasis added)

Given the extreme vulnerability of the average parish's Sunday collection, the APC Committee's recommendations can be likened to rearranging the deck chairs on the *Titanic* as it slipped beneath the waves. They are little more than *window dressing*, all form and no substance. Rather than being written to help parishes protect their revenue, they were written primarily for the purpose of protecting the bishops by *papering* their files! Bishop Schnurr's memorandum and the APC report are, in reality, *smoking-gun* documents; what they do not contain speaks volumes about the authors and their intentions.

In December of 2007, I wrote (p.185) to Francis Cardinal George, the seventh Conference president I would approach. What is unique about Cardinal George is the fact that his Archdiocese (Chicago) is the only archdiocese or diocese I know of that has disseminated what, in effect, are the guidelines I developed in the early 1990s. To his great credit, Cardinal George's then Director of Finance codified and disseminated those guidelines archdiocese-wide in 2005.

I congratulated Cardinal George for having the courage to implement my guidelines, but I also cited a particular embezzlement (described in Chapter IV) as being indicative of a weakness warranting clarification. I also made the connection between the sin of theft and sinful behaviors that flow from that sin. I concluded by stating my belief that the nationwide dissemination and implementation of genuinely secure Sunday collection guidelines would go a long way toward restoring the Church's once premier standing as the face and voice of Christendom.

I was pleased to receive a reply (p.188) from Cardinal George within two weeks of his receiving my letter. He did his best to present an upbeat message, but what it came down to is his contention that "the USCCB cannot legislate for particular dioceses." If you've read this far, you know that's true only because the USCCB has deliberately chosen not to seek Vatican approval of guidelines that would apply to all dioceses and parishes within the Conference's geographic area.

I was particularly struck by the Cardinal's statement: "The Church is not a corporation in this country, and the dioceses are administratively independent of the USCCB." It is as though he and the USCCB feel their not being a "corporation" exempts them from any obligation to protect their assets. Giving him the benefit of the doubt, however, he might have been alluding to the *we-are-not-empowered* defense. In either case, they're both *red herrings*. The U.S. Conference does not need to be a corporation or have administrative control over the dioceses in order to issue a general decree under the provisions of Canon 455; they've done it several times in the past with regard to other matters.[51]

On December 1, 2010, I wrote (p.190) to Cardinal George's successor, Archbishop Timothy M. Dolan, the eighth and final Conference president I approached. I cited several case histories and noted the Conference's apparent valuation of bishops' autonomy above their obligation to protect revenue and, more importantly, to protect the souls entrusted to their care. I also pointed out that the Archdiocese of Chicago codified my Sunday collection guidelines in 2005 and disseminated them archdiocese-wide as a "Best Practice," and that the non-profit National Leadership Roundtable on Church Management (NLRCM) subsequently adopted the Chicago guidelines as a recommended *Best Practice*.

In a reply (p.193) dated December 30, 2010, Archbishop Dolan repeated the USCCB's long-standing mantra, stating: "The USCCB is not authorized to issue a binding decree in this matter." Also mirroring the example of his predecessors, he completely ignored my reference to Canon 455. The fact that not one of the USCCB presidents has ever challenged my contention that Canon Law provides a means by which the USCCB can become empowered to issue a general decree would, in most forums, be deemed a tacit admission that it's true.

This has been the Conference's *modus operandi* from the very beginning: State only the status quo and make no mention of whether or how it could be altered, as that would open the door to questions about why they haven't done so. Quite amazingly, they have successfully employed that subterfuge for decades if not generations. To my great surprise, therefore, that posture changed with my last encounter with a member of the hierarchy.

In his reply, Archbishop Dolan said he was forwarding my letter to Bishop Kevin J. Farrell, Episcopal moderator of the Diocesan Fiscal Management Conference (DFMC), "for his information and study." Wishing to capitalize upon Archbishop Dolan's referral, I wrote (p.194) to Bishop Farrell, on February 3, 2011. I mentioned the DFMC's failure to acknowledge my prior communications, and pointed out the availability of Canon 455 as the means by which the USCCB could implement genuinely secure collection procedures conference-wide.

Imagine my reaction when, in a letter (p.196) dated February 14, 2011, Bishop Farrell declared: "I regret to inform you that your interpretation of Canon 455 is incorrect." To say it took me by surprise would be an understatement. I was floored by his clearly implied declaration that Canon 455 does not provide the USCCB a means for obtaining the Apostolic See's approval to issue a general decree mandating conference-wide guidelines for protecting Sunday collections. In that regard, readers will recall the USCCB's own website includes an *Index of Complementary Norms*, a number of which - by the USCCB's own statement[52] - required and received approval from the Apostolic See in accordance with Canon 455. Further, I have cited Canon 455 in my correspondence with the hierarchy on several occasions dating back to 1999, and not once did any prelate or official challenge or deny its applicability.

Lacking the academic credentials to challenge Bishop Farrell's implied statement that the USCCB cannot avail itself of Canon 455, I sought the opinion of two experts, each possessing a Doctorate in Canon Law. The first expert, Rev. Thomas P. Doyle, O.P., J.C.D., C.A.D.C., stated the USCCB "can make a special law for anything that is not contrary to the general law." Rev. Doyle added that once the proposed decree or law has been formulated, the Conference need only "vote on it and then send it to the Vatican for review and approval."

The second expert, Rev. James A. Coriden, J.C.D., J.D., confirmed Rev. Doyle's opinion, stating, "I can see no reason why Canon 455 could not be employed to issue a set of rules such as you describe. Indeed, one would think that a general decree following upon a special mandate of the Apostolic See pursuant to a request of the conference was tailor-made for such legislation."

In a gesture of fairness to Bishop Farrell and the USCCB, Rev. Coriden speculated that Bishop Farrell might have been implying that the Canon 455 procedure is a "practical impossibility" because the USCCB believes "they couldn't get a two-thirds majority for such legislation, or they think that Rome would not approve it." Rev. Coriden went on to note that the bishops might perceive the proposed guidelines as being "too complex, cumbersome, expensive, or difficult for the great variety of pastoral settings in this country." He added, "Some individual bishops and pastors tend to resist any limitation on their pastoral freedom of action."

Readers will recall from Chapter IV there is essentially only one way to effectively secure the collections, thereby eliminating any need to be concerned about the variety of pastoral settings. Similarly, readers will recall that the secure procedures are not too complex, cumbersome, expensive, or difficult. The procedures are no more or less than what they must be to produce the desired result: an essentially theft-proof Sunday collection.

Having been unequivocally assured of Canon 455's applicability and availability in this matter, I replied (p.197) to Bishop Farrell on March 4, 2011. I summarized the provisions of Canon 455 and asked whether, if the bishops wished, they could avail themselves of those provisions to issue Sunday collection guidelines conference-wide. I apologized for being so persistent, but told him I did not want to ascribe a position to him or to the USCCB that is not completely accurate.

As of the date this manuscript was submitted to the publisher – more than four months after I sent the above letter to Bishop Farrell at both his DFMC and diocesan addresses – no reply had been received. I can only assume he decided he had given me all the attention I deserved and/or that it would be unwise for him to enmesh himself in the matter anymore than he did with his initial reply.

Are insurers asleep at the switch? One might think so. I am amazed that any commercial insurers are or would be willing to indemnify the Church or a particular diocese without requiring them to implement readily available procedures that would prevent virtually all Sunday collection embezzlements. Insurers often pay out large sums of money when an embezzlement is discovered, and many diocesan officials are quick to announce that the loss suffered by the victim parish is being recovered through insurance.

News articles concerning specific embezzlements sometimes include a reference to the stolen funds having been replaced by the diocese acting as its own insurer. Whether such losses are paid for by a commercial insurer or a fund created and maintained by the diocese, however, they are still losses that need not have been sustained. And more importantly, the sins those losses represent are sins that could and should have been prevented.

The Code of Canon Law addresses the subject of insurance as follows:

> Can. 1284 §1. All administrators are bound to fulfill their function with the diligence of a good householder.
>
> §2. Consequently they must:
>
> 1/ exercise vigilance so that the goods entrusted to their care are in no way lost or damaged, taking out insurance policies for this purpose insofar as necessary;

In light of the USCCB's long-standing refusal to take a proactive approach to collection loss prevention, one might assume they keyed on the last part of Canon 1284 §2. 1/ (taking out insurance policies) in the belief that it relieves them from the burden of being particularly concerned about the first part: "exercise vigilance so that the goods entrusted to their care are in no way lost or damaged." Most observers would agree that anyone truly committed to exercising "the diligence of a good householder" would do both, that is, take out insurance *and* exercise vigilance.

As you ponder what you have read in this chapter and, perhaps as well, in your perusal of the letters contained in the appendix of this book, I imagine that, at various points, you found yourself contemplating words such as *evasive, unresponsive,* and *disingenuous.* But whatever thoughts and images came to mind as you read this chapter, I would be very surprised if you concluded the USCCB has not knowingly and willfully shunned the Church-wide implementation of genuinely secure procedures.

At the beginning of this chapter, I made a commitment to be selective about what correspondence I included, limiting it mainly to correspondence directed to and received from Conference presidents and other prelates. While I have largely held to that commitment, I feel that I cannot develop the full scope of the USCCB's nonfeasance without shedding additional light on the Diocesan Fiscal Management Conference (DFMC), the Church's presumed fiscal watchdog. The DFMC is therefore addressed in the next chapter.

Chapter VII

The DFMC, Fiscal Watchdog or Fiscal Lapdog

Visitors to the website of the Diocesan Fiscal Management Conference[53] (DFMC) are met with the following statement:

> Mindful of our special ministry in the Roman Catholic Church as the extension of the Diocesan Bishop in fiscal matters, the members of the Diocesan Fiscal Management Conference unite to be of service to the Church in the Ministry of Fiscal Management.
>
> In particular; this organization promotes the spiritual growth of its members; encourages the development of professional relationships of its members; facilitates the free exchange of ideas and information; and provides fiscal and administrative expertise and professional services to the local and national Church. (emphasis added)

From that brief yet informative statement, we are given the impression the DFMC is actively involved in the fiscal management of the Church in America at all levels. Indeed, how could we not gain that impression? It is clearly stated in what is, in fact, the DFMC's own Mission Statement as contained in its Strategic Plan.[54]

As the official provider of fiscal expertise and professional services to the "national Church," one would naturally assume that one of the DFMC's top priorities, perhaps even its top priority, would be to ensure that the Church's principal source of revenue is being adequately protected *Church-wide*. We can infer from my twenty-plus years of correspondence with various USCCB and DFMC officials, however, that the DFMC has been prohibited, either expressly or *sub rosa,* from delving into that area.

Clearly, the DFMC membership is comprised of highly intelligent men and women, many of them CPAs who, I can only assume, strive to fulfill the commitments delineated in the DFMC's mission statement. For them, therefore, the realization that they have been barred from addressing an area of such vital importance to the Church must be extremely disheartening, especially since the reason given for the USCCB's inaction is as superficial as the vast majority of readers have no doubt concluded it is.

Some might find it difficult to fault the DFMC and its membership for their apparent failure to act, but I'm not among that number. I firmly believe their silence and inaction amount to complicity and have been instrumental in the USCCB's thus far very successful, decades-old strategy for keeping the issue of Sunday collection security out of their lap. The fact that the DFMC leadership has so often either completely ignored my correspondence or replied without addressing the points I raised is, to me, a good indicator of guilty knowledge. The DFMC leadership knows I have been attempting to instigate the plowing of heretofore forbidden ground, but rather than come right out and admit that, as a group, they are prohibited from addressing Sunday collection security, they simply opted to ignore me.

On April 29, 2005, the DFMC Board of Directors adopted a document entitled "Standards for Ethical Behavior & Professional Conduct."[55] The stated purpose of the document is "to demonstrate the commitment of the DFMC to preserving high ethical standards among its membership and to remind membership of its special degree of accountability as faithful servants of the Church." We see in the Introduction this statement: "It is our vocation to care for the Church as 'a good householder.'" The reference to "a good householder" is taken from Canon 1284, Section 1, which reads as follows: "All administrators are bound to fulfill their function with the diligence of a good householder."[56] Canon 1284 goes on to state that administrators must "exercise vigilance so that the goods entrusted to their care are in no way lost or damaged."

Among the twenty-six "Core Values" enunciated in the DFMC "Standards for Ethical Behavior & Professional Conduct," the seventh reads in pertinent part as follows: "We seek to utilize the best business practices to further the work of the Church." In twenty-first place is this Core Value: "We will implement policies and procedures to protect the resources of the Church from fraud, misuse and waste, and to provide accurate and reliable financial reporting." And in twenty-fourth place we have this Core Value: "We will endeavor to fully inform the leadership of the Church, particularly when information might influence or modify a decision. Further, we will strive to advise the leadership of the options pertaining to a given issue."

With all of those high-sounding pronouncements, one can only wonder how the DFMC can ignore the nationwide vulnerability of the Church's primary source of income and still maintain they are:

preserving high ethical standards among their membership,

functioning with the diligence of a good householder,

utilizing the best business practices.

implementing policies and procedures to protect the resources of the Church from fraud, misuse and waste,

fully informing the leadership of the Church, particularly when information might influence or modify a decision, and

advising the leadership of the options pertaining to a given issue.

Frankly, if it weren't so tragic, it would be humorous. Countless souls are being damaged, perhaps even lost, due to the sin of theft, not to mention the sins those thefts finance, virtually all of which could be ended by actually following "the best business practices" and implementing readily available "policies and procedures to protect the resources of the Church from fraud, misuse and waste."

With that as a background, it will be helpful to the reader to gain some insight into the efforts that failed to convince the DFMC to initiate action with a view toward eliminating the Sunday collection's extreme vulnerability. In Chapter VI, I described correspondence had with the then NCCB Director of Finance, Sister Frances Mlocek. Readers will recall that she referred my letter and enclosures to the Administrator of the DFMC in 1990. I subsequently directed a letter (p.199) to that individual, expressing my concern for the collections' extreme vulnerability, and offering to assist in any effort to resolve that issue.

The Administrator did not respond to my letter, thereby causing me to send a follow-up letter (p.201) two months later. In that letter, I mentioned collection procedures, including the use of numbered bag seals and transmittal forms. I suggested the Administrator consider initiating a pilot program to determine the best way to secure the collections. Once again, he did not respond.

Concurrent with the above letter to the Administrator, I sent a second letter (p.203) to Sister Mlocek. In that letter, I noted that the collection embezzlements that come to light are only "the tip of the iceberg," and that nationwide losses have to be "staggering." I ended the letter stating, "We close churches, and worse yet - schools, for mainly financial reasons, but no one seems willing to lift a finger to curtail the cash losses everyone knows or should know are occurring each and every Sunday of the year."

Sister Mlocek replied stating the DFMC referral she had given me was among the best she could give, but also noted I was free to contact diocesan fiscal managers. To facilitate that, she provided a set of labels for use in any mailing I might wish to make. As I could not see myself cajoling 195 individual fiscal managers *and* their prelates into implementing secure Sunday collection procedures, I did not follow up on Sister Mlocek's suggestion.

As I mentioned earlier, the DFMC Administrator never acknowledged my correspondence. Consequently, I redirected my attention to the NCCB (now the USCCB), this time in the person of its president as detailed in the preceding chapter. Even then, however, I did not give up on the potential for making progress through Sister Mlocek or the DFMC. I wrote to Sister Mlocek on two additional occasions, the most recent being in November of 1993. Sister Mlocek replied on January 3, 1994, advising that the issue of Sunday collection security "is simply not a topic and task which I can, or should address. This concern lies within the domain of local bishops and diocesan fiscal managers." She went on to advise that she was forwarding my comments to the Executive Director of the DFMC, a clergyman with a doctorate in Education.

I wrote (p.205) to that individual in January of 1994, referencing Sister Mlocek and the files she had forwarded to him on my behalf. I outlined the background of my failed efforts to work with individual pastors, and I offered to share my insight and experience with the DFMC at its next annual meeting. The Executive Director did not reply to my letter, and it was at this point (in 1994) that I stopped trying to make contact with the DFMC. Fourteen years later, however, and as readers will recall from the last chapter, Cardinal George recommended I correspond with a specific DFMC member who he said "has brought together a committee that has begun to create guidelines for accounting practices and financial services in the dioceses in the United States."

On February 1, 2008, I directed a letter (p.208) to that individual, the CFO of an east coast diocese. In my letter, I mentioned Cardinal George's referral and asked (quoting Cardinal George) "to be part of the conversation as it moves forward in shaping guidelines that will change our practices in this country in the years to come." Notwithstanding the fact that I was writing to the CFO at the suggestion of the President of the USCCB who had also copied the individual with his (Cardinal George's) letter to me, I failed to receive even the courtesy of an acknowledgment.

After waiting nearly six months for a reply, I once again wrote (p.211) to Cardinal George, noting the CFO's failure to reply, and what I described as the nexus between vulnerable Sunday collection funds and the ability of wayward priests (and lay-persons) to fund their aberrant behaviors. I ended the letter, stating my opinion that the Church remains in a downward spiral due, in large part, to the hierarchy's refusal to effectively address difficult issues such as Sunday collection security. My prose was rewarded with a preprinted note card acknowledging receipt of my letter; the Cardinal never replied.

On August 15, 2008, I directed a letter (p.213) to the then DFMC President, seeking to draw his attention to the issue. I asked him if he could explain why neither the USCCB nor the DFMC has moved to develop and implement uniformly secure procedures for protecting Sunday collection funds nationwide. I called his attention to the DFMC's commitment to "implement policies and procedures to protect the resources of the Church from fraud, misuse and waste," and said I can imagine no higher calling for the DFMC than to ensure the existence and application of a genuinely effective level of security over the Church's primary source of income, the Sunday collection.

The DFMC President did not reply to my letter. Nevertheless, I decided to make one final effort to prod the DFMC into action via email, the most recent of which was sent on February 22, 2009 to fourteen of fifteen people then constituting its Board of Directors. The fifteenth member was the Board's then long-time Episcopal Moderator, Donald W. Trautman, Bishop of the Diocese of Erie, Pennsylvania, who, if he deigned to reply, would no doubt have repeated the USCCB's *we-are-not-empowered* mantra. My confidence in that regard was partly based upon a review of his Diocese's *Parish Financial Practices Policy Manual*[57] which contains so little guidance on the handling of collections that it is virtually useless.

In my email (p.216) I began by referencing an earlier email that had been directed to thirteen members of the DFMC Board of Directors and failed to elicit even one reply. The second email can best be described as a broadside that should have elicited a barrage of indignant replies. In spite of the fact the email was sent to fourteen

DFMC Board members, all but one at their home diocese, not one of them acknowledged receipt, let alone offered a substantive reply. To say the USCCB keeps the DFMC membership on a short leash would be a gross understatement.

Interestingly, however, the day after I sent that email, the CFO I had written more than one year earlier, and whose failure to reply I specifically mentioned in my email to the DFMC Board members, penned a reply (p.220) to my then year-old letter. The CFO apologized for the delay in responding to my letter and went on to explain that his committee's primary purpose is to "represent the U.S. Catholic Church before regulatory bodies in the formulation of accounting principles and reporting standards that affect the Catholic Church." He advised that my letter would be retained for future reference and would be considered "a resource for developing sound parish offertory procedures."

In my reply (p.221) I expressed my astonishment at the almost total lack of concern the DFMC has for the Church's principal source of revenue. I noted he had mentioned representing the Church before the American Institute of Certified Public Accountants (AICPA) and I asked how he or any member of the DFMC could be comfortable doing so, knowing the Church's principal source of revenue has been afforded <u>none</u> of the protections called for by the AICPA's own standards. I also brought out the connection between Sunday collection embezzlements and the abuse scandal, and called upon the CFO to urge the DFMC Board to issue a "white paper" that I said "could well provide the USCCB leadership with an incentive to stop dissembling and do the right thing." Bottom line, I didn't pull any punches. I even copied Cardinal George so the USCCB would be hard pressed to play dumb. Nevertheless, neither the committee chairman nor Cardinal George replied.

The title of this chapter, *Fiscal Watchdog or Fiscal Lapdog*, was not chosen for its comic appeal, but rather because it poses a serious question. Does the Diocesan Fiscal Management Conference really "implement policies and procedures to protect the resources of the Church from fraud, misuse and waste"[58] as they claim, or do they merely *dance* to the *music* played by the U.S. Conference of Catholic Bishops, no matter how out of tune that music might be. From all appearances, I fear the only *watchdog* within the DFMC is its Episcopal Moderator who, as can be inferred from his letter (p.194) referenced toward the end of Chapter VI, presides over the Conference to ensure that its members do not stray into forbidden territory.

Chapter VIII

Guilty or Not Guilty - You Decide

He said to his disciples,
'Things that cause sin will inevitably occur,
but woe to the person through whom they occur.'
Luke 17:1

Fourth and last on the list of particulars I undertook to establish beyond reasonable doubt is that the failure of the U.S. Conference of Catholic Bishops to implement genuinely secure procedures renders them ultimately responsible for virtually every loss of Sunday collection funds due to embezzlement as well as for the moral lapses of those who succumb (usually weekly) to the temptation presented by a vulnerable collection system. I also stated that responsibility for those losses has rested with the USCCB for at least the past thirty-five years. If you find that difficult to accept, allow me to put it into perspective.

In the heyday of the railroads, The Wilson Company of Chicago, Illinois, published a periodical entitled *The Railway Age*. That publication served as a medium through which the various railroad owners and administrators shared information regarding current events, common problems and new technologies and procedures, including those affecting the security of goods carried by the railroads. Two articles contained in the January 3, 1908 issue (yes, that's 1908, it's not a typo) are particularly relevant.

The first article concerns the development of a serially numbered railroad car seal. According to the manufacturer, Automatic Car Seal Company of Detroit, Michigan, the seal was "designed to furnish positive protection, in that the seal once snapped in place cannot be opened without destroying it, and when broken a new one cannot be substituted without the fact being apparent."[59] (emphasis added)

An illustration of the 1908 seal is shown on the next page. Note how closely it resembles the modern, tamper-proof numbered seal pictured below it.

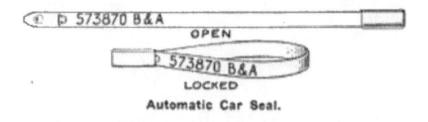

1908 Serially-numbered Railroad Car Seal

Modern-day Serially-numbered Tamper-proof Seal

So here we have an early twentieth-century vendor who recognized the need for "positive protection" *and* created a device to provide that protection. In stark contrast - and fully one hundred years later - we have the hierarchy of the Catholic Church in America who, from all indications, have yet to recognize and act upon that very same need. Compounding the hierarchy's failure to act, especially since the 1950s or thereabouts, is the fact that all they needed to do was adopt the common-sense procedures described in Chapter IV along with what, by then, was an inexpensive and readily available security device.

The second article concerns what, for religious leaders, should be of even greater importance: the elimination of a temptation to sin. The same issue of *The Railway Age* contains a letter to the editors submitted by an unnamed railroad's claims department. The letter is entitled "The Sealing of Cars" and concerns losses resulting from thefts of goods in transit. More specifically, the letter notes the ease with which old style seals could be opened and closed "without leaving evidence of having been tampered with." It goes on to state, in pertinent part:

> Officials freely admit that much pilfering from cars is committed by employees. What protection, then, is secured from the use of station numbers on seals, when an employee can seal a car, break that seal, rob the car and reseal it with an exact duplicate of the broken seal, including the number? <u>Is it any wonder that employees go wrong when such opportunities are so apparent, and should such temptations be placed before them</u>?[60] (emphasis added)

No, your eyes are not deceiving you; a railroad claims department actually recognized in 1908 what the hierarchy of the Catholic Church in America has apparently yet to recognize more than one hundred years later, that is, that the temptation to steal should not be placed (or knowingly left) before anyone. And if the USCCB were to claim they realize the wrongness and danger of unnecessary temptation, it must then be said they have failed to act upon that realization in any meaningful way. Generally speaking, the average church's Sunday collection is as vulnerable to repetitive theft in 2011 as it was in 1911. Consequently, the temptation to steal from the Sunday collection is as great today as it was fully one hundred years ago.

From the two articles cited above, it can be seen that the hierarchy could, in fact, have implemented secure procedures as long ago as the early 1900s. For various reasons, however, I'm more comfortable dating the beginning of their knowing and willful nonfeasance to the mid-seventies. The main reason for that is the fact that the American Institute of Certified Public Accountants did not issue their *Statement on Auditing Standards*[61] until 1973. Add a couple of years to allow time for those standards to have circulated within the accounting profession, and we're looking at a period of nonfeasance totaling approximately thirty-five years.

The Church's hierarchical structure is at the root of the seemingly incomprehensible absence of adequate measures to protect the Church's primary source of income. Each diocese and archdiocese is essentially a fiefdom under the exclusive control of its prelate who might be a bishop, an archbishop or a cardinal. Regardless of a prelate's rank within the hierarchy, however, he is lord and master over the diocese placed in his personal care by the Church's supreme leader, the Pope. As one can easily imagine, such absolute power is not willingly shared with or ceded to other authority, not even to the USCCB to which all of the Catholic bishops in America belong. Still, one would assume the bishops could appreciate and agree upon the need for conference-wide procedures that would virtually guarantee the safety of the Church's principal source of revenue. Sadly, however, the facts brought out in this book clearly establish that such an assumption would be incorrect.

As readers well know at this juncture, the reason most frequently invoked by the USCCB in defense of their failure to act is that they are not empowered to mandate how the collections must be handled within individual dioceses. What they have always left unsaid and refuse to address, however, is the fact that the Code of Canon Law provides conferences such as the USCCB a means of becoming so empowered. As noted in Chapter V, as well as in several of my letters to members of the hierarchy, Canon 455 §1 states: "A conference of bishops can only issue general decrees in cases where universal law has prescribed it or a special mandate of the Apostolic See has established it either motu proprio [on the Pope's initiative] <u>or at the request of the conference itself</u>."[62] (parenthetic explanation and emphasis added)

In light of the above, it is apparent the USCCB's failure to utilize Canon 455 to issue a general decree implementing secure collection procedures conference-wide cannot be attributed to a lack of authority; clearly, that authority is theirs for the asking. Rather, their failure is attributable to a conscious decision on the part of several successive USCCB administrations not to seek that authority, thereby keeping responsibility for the security of the collections subject to the varied opinions and judgments of 195 individual prelates and their respective staffs. As I speculated earlier, the USCCB's intransigence might have something to do with Section 2 of Canon 455 which states:

> The decrees mentioned in §1, in order to be enacted validly in a plenary meeting, <u>must be passed by at least a two-thirds vote of the prelates</u> who belong to the conference and possess a deliberative vote. They do not obtain binding force unless they have been legitimately promulgated after having been reviewed by the Apostolic See.[63] (emphasis added)

One would certainly think at least two-thirds of the prelates can and would recognize *and* act upon the fiscal and moral imperatives involved in this particular matter, but the Conference's apparent failure to seek authority to act conference-wide strongly suggests its leaders do not share that opinion. Measured against the backdrop of the enormous presence of sin, abuse and monetary loss that have been documented in this book, we are only left to wonder why the USCCB has failed to act on this issue and, more specifically, why they have gone to such great lengths to avoid implementing readily available, low-cost procedures that would put a virtual end to what is clearly a morally and fiscally unacceptable state of affairs.

In any event, the seriousness of the USCCB's failure to act is not mitigated by any secular considerations or fear of potentially embarrassing publicity. The U.S. Conference of Catholic Bishops has knowingly and willfully failed to do what ought to be done, and the depth and breadth of their failure might well constitute the most widespread and longest running case of organizational nonfeasance ever documented.

Chapter IX

Where do we go from here?

It is written:
'My house shall be a house of prayer,'
but you are making it a den of thieves.
Matthew 21:13

Although I have often wondered why my twenty-plus years of communication with members of the hierarchy seem to have fallen upon so many deaf ears, I remain at somewhat of a loss to explain it. It is quite possible those officials with whom I have communicated viewed my status as an ordinary member of the flock to be an automatic disqualifier. While college educated, I do lack an advanced degree or certification such as an MBA or CPA, and I can therefore understand how my call for reform would, at least initially, have been viewed with doubt or suspicion.

Still, my communications were not without substantial underpinnings, frequently containing citations from authoritative sources such as the American Institute of Certified Public Accountants, the Code of Canon Law and the Holy Bible. One would think those three sources would especially resonate with my target audience which is comprised of the very same people who study and apply the standards and principles contained in those sources. Indeed, I have no doubt one or more of the prelates I have written to over the past twenty-plus years had a hand in crafting portions of the present Code of Canon Law.

Only once in the past twenty-plus years did any bishop, archbishop or cardinal challenge or dispute the accuracy or applicability of my citations. The lone exception, as readers will recall from the latter part of Chapter VI, came from the Episcopal Moderator of the DFMC who asserted that my "interpretation" of Canon 455 was "incorrect," thereby implying the USCCB is somehow prohibited from utilizing the empowering provisions of that canon. Readers will also recall, however, that two canon law experts subsequently confirmed the USCCB can, if it so desires, utilize the empowering provisions of Canon 455 to issue Sunday collection guidelines conference-wide.

My credentials aside, what do we say about prominent lay persons such as Oklahoma Governor Frank Keating who, upon undertaking to chair (at the USCCB President's request) the Church's National Review Board, discovered his extensive qualifications and experience were no match for the Church's entrenched bureaucracy. Being the self-respecting, honorable man he is, Governor Keating did what most people of his caliber and stature would do: he resigned in protest rather than countenance the stonewalling conduct of certain prelates.

Consider also Rev. Thomas P. Doyle, J.C.D., C.A.D.C., a Dominican priest with a Pontifical Doctorate in Canon Law and five separate master's degrees,[64] who sacrificed a rising career at the Vatican Embassy in Washington, DC, to become an outspoken advocate for clergy sexual abuse victims. In 1985, Rev. Doyle spearheaded the development of a report entitled "The Problem of Sexual Molestation by Roman Catholic Clergy: Meeting the Problem in a Comprehensive and Responsible Manner."[65] That report was a direct result of a growing realization on the part of Rev. Doyle and others, including a lay attorney and the founder of St. Luke's Institute (a facility for the treatment of sexually troubled priests), that sexual molestation of children by members of the clergy was widespread and thus in need of conference-wide attention. What followed their presentation of that report clearly illustrates that the USCCB's nonfeasance isn't attributable to the messenger. Rather, their failure to act lies with the message and whether that message is one the USCCB wishes to hear.

Here is how Louise I. Gerdes, author of "Child Sexual Abuse in the Catholic Church,"[66] described the reception given the report submitted by Rev. Doyle and his associates:

> In view of the escalating scandal and the multimillion-dollar legal actions, all three urged Catholic leaders to take strong and effective action to deal with the impending crisis. In the autumn of 1985, U.S. bishops discussed the report in secret sessions at their semiannual gathering. However, the bishops would only commit to deal with cases of child sexual abuse as they arose in each diocese. Creating a nationwide church policy on child sexual abuse, the bishops believed, ran against the essential

<u>autonomy of each bishop</u> in his diocese. When Doyle spoke publicly about the report and the problem of clergy child sexual abuse, many bishops were offended, and Doyle's career as a Vatican representative ended.[67] (emphasis added)

Sounds familiar, yes? Do you see the *divide and conquer* strategy in the USCCB's handling of that matter? The strategy is quite simple: keep responsibility for corrective action out of the USCCB's lap so that 195 prelates can continue to do whatever they wish. Note also the reference to a bishop's "autonomy." As often as that word (or its equivalent) has been invoked, one could easily conclude autonomy is a bishop's most prized faculty.

In the case of Rev. Doyle's report, the bishops placed the preservation of their individual autonomy ahead of an opportunity to create a uniformly safer environment for vulnerable youth conference-wide. Regarding the subject of this book, the USCCB has repeatedly placed the preservation of bishops' autonomy ahead of the opportunity to ensure the fiscal and moral wellbeing of the Church. If we could rewrite the bible verse shown at the beginning of this chapter, Jesus would be admonishing the bishops thusly: "It is written: 'My house shall be a house of prayer,' but you have *kept it* a den of thieves."

To employ an often-used sports analogy, the ball is in the hierarchy's court. For generations, they have ignored and evaded the issue of Sunday collection embezzlement and, even today, apparently believe their interests are best served by continuing on that path. As a result, the best interests of Christ's Church and the faithful (including those who fall into sin due, in large part, to the average collection's great vulnerability) have been relegated to the proverbial *back burner*, and they will remain there unless and until the U.S. Conference of Catholic Bishops is *forced* to address the issue in a proactive manner.

The information and correspondence contained in this book make it abundantly clear the conference-wide implementation of a genuinely secure Sunday collection system will require far greater pressure than the author has been able to exert over the past two decades. Sadly, and much like the sexual abuse scandal, I am convinced that rectification of this glaring deficiency will ultimately require intense and prolonged coverage in the mainstream media. And that will not come to pass without the aid of *many* committed and concerned Catholics who find the USCCB's disdainful treatment of this issue as outrageous and unacceptable as I do.

All such Catholics are therefore urged, even implored, to join this quest for accountability. Souls are being damaged *and* lost for no other reason than to preserve the secular autonomy of one hundred ninety-five prelates. Scripture does not indicate Jesus acted to stop Judas' thievery from the Apostles' purse (John 12:6). In that situation, however, it seems reasonable to assume Judas was left to his own ends because of the role he was to play in the fulfillment of the scriptures. Today's Sunday collection thieves play no such role. Their thefts serve no purpose other than to corrupt their own souls and further weaken the Church's fiscal health, already in great jeopardy as evidenced by the number of dioceses that have declared bankruptcy in recent years.

Whether you act at the parish, diocesan, archdiocesan or national level, this vital cause can use every last ounce of support it can muster. Toward that end, I offer this concluding communication.

MEMORANDUM

DATE: Sunday, June 12, 2011

TO: Members of the U.S. Conference of Catholic Bishops

FROM: The U.S. Catholic Laity

SUBJECT: Fiscal and Moral Accountability

The time for you, the U.S. Conference of Catholic Bishops, to act decisively to correct the extreme vulnerability of the Church's principal source of income is long past. Whether you realize it or not, the USCCB is repeating the errors of judgment that caused a minimum 15-year delay in your response to the sexual abuse crisis which, you will recall, was credibly brought to your attention in 1985.

Although nothing can compare to the sexual abuse crisis in terms of lives damaged (many irreparably) and faith lost, your failure to provide an adequate level of protection for the Church's principal source of income is a very close second. This is especially so when you consider that easy access to Sunday collection funds facilitated the evil acts of an untold number of abusers.

While the USCCB is not presently empowered to direct how the collections must be handled within its member dioceses, Canon 455 clearly provides you with the means of becoming empowered. The fact that you have refused to seek that authority accrues to your everlasting dishonor, and each passing week only adds to your moral deficit.

Recall Jesus' words: *"Things that cause sin will inevitably occur, but woe to the person through whom they occur."* The time for you to cease all evasiveness is at hand. Act now, and do what you surely know ought to be done. Show us that your actions embody and personify the Church's teachings.

Appendix

This appendix contains much of the correspondence the author has had with the hierarchy of the Catholic Church. Each of these letters is referred to and summarized in either Chapter VI or Chapter VII. They have been placed here so that those who find the summaries satisfactory are not *forced* to read the letters. To facilitate access to a specific letter, however, each summary includes the page number where the letter can be found and read.

[letterhead]

January 18, 1990

Sister Frances Mlocek, IHM
Director of Finance
N.C.C.B./U.S.C.C.
3211 Fourth Street, NE
Washington, DC 20017-1194

Dear Sister Mlocek:

Enclosed is a treatise/proposal concerning the Church's primary source of revenue, the Sunday collection. Approximately two months ago, I furnished a similar proposal to [name withheld], Chancellor of the Archdiocese of Boston. I firmly believe the subject is national in scope and importance, however, hence my referral to you at this time.

By way of introduction, I am a retired Postal Executive and most recently served as Postal Inspector in Charge of the Boston Division (1982-1986). In that capacity, I was responsible for overseeing all USPS audit, criminal and security matters in the New England states. I have over 30 years experience in various aspects of postal finance and security operations, including the assessment of internal security systems and procedures.

Over the course of my career, I and my family have resided in several locations, including Washington, DC. Consequently, I've had the opportunity to observe, albeit unofficially, the manner in which various parishes handle their Sunday collection, and I consistently found them to be highly deficient in the area of internal security. Obviously, this condition did not arise overnight; to my knowledge, the Church has not materially altered Sunday collection procedures in decades if not generations.

Your first inclination, Sister Mlocek, may be to label this presentation as the brainchild of an overzealous member of the flock. Our Church would not be well served by such a response, however, and I therefore urge you to give it the most careful reading your busy schedule will permit; the financial wellbeing of the American Catholic Church deserves no less.

I will be pleased to elaborate on any aspect of my proposal and answer any questions you may have as a result of your review. I can be reached by telephone at 781-821-0412.

Very truly yours,

Michael W. Ryan

[letterhead]

November 13, 1990

PERSONAL AND CONFIDENTIAL
Daniel E. Pilarczyk, President
National Conference of Catholic Bishops
3211 Fourth Street, NE
Washington, DC 20017-1194

Dear Bishop Pilarczyk:

Enclosed is a copy of a letter I directed to Cardinal Law this date. Copies of previous correspondence between me, His Eminence and then Chancellor [name withheld] are attached. Since then, I have also been in contact with the current Chancellor, your Director of Finance and the Administrator of the Diocesan Fiscal Management Conference.

Quite simply, Eminence, when it comes to revenue protection, the Roman Catholic Church in the United States is operating out of its hip pocket. Just think how much more she could do for the needy and homeless, both here and abroad, if those in authority would accept and respond to the fact that millions of dollars are being surreptitiously taken from the Sunday collection every year in this country.

[NOTE: A paragraph contained in the original letter was removed because it is completely unrelated to the issue this book is intended to address]

I was employed with the federal government for 32 years, Eminence, and I know how difficult it can be to achieve a desired course of action. I also know, however, that it can be done if proper direction and a sense of urgency are conveyed from the top. Needless to say, that's where you come into the picture. As you can tell, I feel strongly about these issues, and I trust my efforts in calling them to your attention will not be in vain.

Very truly yours,

Michael W. Ryan

[letterhead]

November 30, 1992

Archbishop Thomas J. Murphy
Chairman, Committee on Stewardship
National Conference of Catholic Bishops
3211 Fourth Street, NE
Washington, DC 20017-1194

Dear Archbishop Murphy:

Congratulations on your selection to serve as Chairman of the Ad Hoc Committee on Stewardship. Based upon recent news accounts, the Church's fiscal condition is clearly a major area of concern. The existence of a pastoral letter notwithstanding, I would like to suggest that you give particular attention to a facet of fiscal soundness which, to my knowledge, has yet to be seriously addressed by the hierarchy of today's Church.

The area I am referring to is Security. More specifically, I mean security over the Church's single most important source of revenue: the Sunday collection. Believe it or not, this nearly 2000-year-old mode of Church support is no safer today than it was when JOHN (12.6) named Judas as the Church's first embezzler. Indeed, it's even more vulnerable today, in that several persons have lone, unobserved and undetectable access to the collection funds or a portion thereof in virtually every parish.

In a relevant aside, Archbishop Murphy, I'd like to explore the term "Stewardship". My 1959 Webster's Unabridged defines a steward as: "1. a man entrusted with the management of the household or estate of another; one employed to manage the domestic affairs, superintend the servants, collect the rents or income, keep the accounts, etc. 2. one who acts as a supervisor or administrator, as of finances or property, for another or others." Assuming those definitions have not been totally eclipsed by a later, more authoritative edition, it seems to me the Committee on Stewardship should, at least, give equal attention to the hierarchy's performance vis-a-vis its obligation to "collect the ... income" and be a responsible "administrator ... of finances." I respectfully postulate that the hierarchy has not acted in a responsible manner in the past and is not presently so acting.

I'm sure you're personally aware of past incidents of theft from collection funds in your own Archdiocese. As an outsider, I am nevertheless aware of several such cases covered in east coast newspapers; imagine how many more there must be that were never made public! You may find it distasteful, but I'm enclosing a news transcript regarding the pastor of an east coast parish; it clearly illustrates not only what can and does happen in the absence of a secure Sunday Collection system but also just how ill-equipped the hierarchy is to even recognize a blatant theft situation, let alone confront and resolve such a problem.

It's really quite simple, Archbishop Murphy. If the Church hasn't implemented any systems or procedures for providing even a minimally acceptable level of security for the Sunday collection (It hasn't!), the only thefts that will ever surface are those that are discovered by accident or chance. And of that number, only a fraction make the newspapers. Let's face it, how many parishioners would feel good about continuing their support, if they learned their $50 to $100 monthly offering was only going to make up for the $100 to $500 some trusted employee or volunteer was stealing every week! Pastors are well aware of this and are extremely sensitive to its ramifications.

I'm not a statistician, but I believe the so-called Law of Averages and the theory of statistical probability would support a figure of 5% to 10% as an estimate of the number of parishes being affected by ongoing embezzlements at any given time. Just think what that might convert to on an annual basis. To say we're talking millions of dollars would not be an exaggeration! It seems to me, Archbishop Murphy, the hierarchy ought to focus its collective attention on the elimination of that "shrinkage" problem before it dares to ask the Faithful to give even more.

In a recent letter to Cardinal Law - this is not my maiden voyage into Church affairs - I advised him a Sunday collection system can only be deemed secure if pertinent security procedures and equipment are applied so that no one - not even the pastor - has lone, unobserved and undetectable access to those funds. Further, that mantle of protection must begin immediately after the collection is taken up (when it's consolidated at the rear of the church) and must remain absolutely unbroken until all funds have been properly deposited in the parish bank account.

At the risk of being irreverent, I also told Cardinal Law I believe the hierarchy doesn't want to terminate pastors' access to undeposited collection funds. But in keeping those funds accessible to pastors, they are also exposing them to others, some of whom have zero qualms about making covert deductions. It's a distasteful subject, to be sure, but then so is abortion and pedophilia; none of these evils will disappear by themselves. Significant positive action is clearly required!

If you and your committee decide to acknowledge and confront this formidable and ongoing drain on Church revenue, Archbishop Murphy, I would be pleased to furnish you a copy of my handbook, "Protecting the Purse". It contains the rationale and detailed guidelines for moving the Sunday collection out of the "at risk" category and protecting it all the way to the bank. No matter what, you have my best wishes for success in this critical task!

Most Sincerely,

Michael W. Ryan

[letterhead]

December 28, 1992

<u>PERSONAL AND CONFIDENTIAL</u>
Archbishop Thomas J. Murphy
Chairman, NCCB Committee on Stewardship
Archdiocese of Seattle
910 Marion Street
Seattle, WA 98104-1299

Dear Archbishop Murphy:

Thank you for your prompt reply to my letter of November 30 concerning the NCCB Ad Hoc Committee on Stewardship. It's good to hear that you deem the letter of sufficient import to warrant sharing its contents with your fellow committee members.

My knowledge of the incidence of collection embezzlement is largely limited to those cases I come across in the newspapers. The hierarchy, however, knows of all <u>reported</u> embezzlements and thereby has a much greater database to draw upon for statistical projections. Nevertheless, one must also consider the existence of embezzlements which are discovered at the local parish level but never reported. It's quite possible that number exceeds the number reported to local Bishops and, when they're all combined, it wouldn't surprise me to learn that, at any point in time, 10% of all Sunday collections are suffering ongoing embezzlements.

Why am I dwelling on this? It's quite simple: to drive home the point that the U. S. Catholic Church is easily losing tens - <u>probably hundreds</u> - of millions of dollars <u>annually</u>, because the hierarchy has somehow failed to recognize the depth and scope of the problem or, having recognized it, concluded that it is more important to give pastors free rein (including ongoing access to <u>undeposited</u> collection funds) than it is to resolve the problem. In either case, preservation of the status quo is unacceptable. With your forbearance, I will underscore my point by recounting for you the results of what, to date, constitutes the only known implementation of the collection security system I developed.

I belong to a suburban parish whose Sunday collection was running about 3% <u>under</u> SPLY for the first 3 months of calendar year 1992; that was consistent with data for the Archdiocese of Boston as a whole. For reasons I will not go into at this time, I had been greatly concerned about the safety of our collection for several years. Anyway, after much cajoling by me, the pastor finally agreed to implement my security system. Well, beginning with start-up day on the first Sunday of April, a very striking turnaround occurred.

As of the end of October, the collection was averaging about 8% <u>over</u> SPLY and <u>cash</u>, which was running 8.5% <u>under</u> SPLY, tallied more than 15% <u>over</u> SPLY for the 7-month period ending October 31!

There could be more than one explanation for this phenomenon, but a rise of only 4% in check donations (they were basically even with SPLY for Jan-Mar) while cash donations went from 8.5% <u>under</u> to more than 15% <u>over</u> SPLY, makes it all but impossible to avoid the obvious conclusion. For emphasis, however, just compare our 1991 Easter/Christmas collections (<u>before</u> secure procedures were implemented) with those for 1992.

	Christmas & Easter 1991	Christmas & Easter 1992	Difference	% Change
Currency	$ 7,997.00	$14,119.00	+ $6,122.00	+ 76.5%
Checks	15,660.00	16,604.00	+ 944.00	+ 6.0%
Coin	184.50	163.00	- 21.50	- 11.7%
Total	$23,841.50	$30,886.00	+ $7,044.50	+ 29.5%

The comparison almost shouts at you, doesn't it? I do ask, however, that this information not result in any type of missive to the Archdiocese of Boston. I have already communicated with Cardinal Law regarding this trend, and don't want my pastor to be embarrassed, disciplined or made the subject of an inquiry. He's the only pastor in the Archdiocese of Boston who can now look his parishioners in the eye and <u>knowledgeably</u> say that each and every dollar they place in the basket on Sunday gets to the bank!

I've done my share of head-butting both with and within the federal bureaucracy over the years, Bishop Murphy, and I know how hard it is to "sell" the need for change. Acceptance of even the most obvious improvements is agonizingly slow to reach fruition. Regarding security over the Sunday collection, the benefits to be gained are <u>clearly</u> significant, even though estimates may vary. At the risk of sounding smug, I know I have the answer! But the question is: Is our Church finally ready to face the reality of the situation <u>and</u> do what must be done to correct it? Frankly, my prior experiences with the Archdiocese of Boston, the Diocese of Providence, and the NCCB do not leave me at all optimistic.

My motivation for developing a collection security handbook was not pecuniary. I have an ample retirement income and could spend the rest of my life in idleness. But I feel strongly about the issue, and wrote the handbook after repeated overtures to the hierarchy were spurned, making it clear that help for individual parishes would have to circumvent the hierarchy. While I can't afford to give the handbook away, I would be more than willing to collaborate with you and/or your committee. Naturally, my offer presupposes that your group reaches the point of recognizing and confronting the collection security problem. In any event, know that you have my best wishes for success in this vital mission.

Most Sincerely,

Michael W. Ryan

[letterhead]

December 15, 1992

<u>PERSONAL AND CONFIDENTIAL</u>
Most Reverend Alfred C. Hughes
Vicar General & Curia Moderator
Archdiocese of Boston
2121 Commonwealth Avenue
Boston, MA 02135—3193

Dear Bishop Hughes:

I received your letter of December 4 concerning my letters of October 27 and November 20, 1992. In my November 20 letter to Cardinal Law, I made a commitment (absent any positive response) to discontinue my efforts to reach him directly. Naturally, that commitment was predicated upon the supposition that Cardinal Law would read my letter. Ergo, it's important to me to know whether you received my November 20 letter from the Cardinal himself or from his secretary and, if from his secretary (or someone else), whether or not His Eminence actually read it. A great deal of correspondence for top officials never reaches them, and I don't wish to draw any inferences on the basis of erroneous input.

> [Author's note: Two paragraphs that appeared here in the original letter were removed due to the fact they are completely unrelated to the subject of this book.]

I've also noted an interesting characteristic that seems to run through virtually all of the correspondence I have ever received from Church officials. It is an almost complete avoidance of any specific language that would identify the precise nature of the topic(s) raised in my correspondence. For example, I have made numerous references to <u>theft</u> and <u>embezzlement</u> in prior letters and have even furnished news transcripts dealing with the same terms, but they have been meticulously avoided in all replies.

I specifically related a recent occurrence which would seem to indicate implementation of secure Sunday collection procedures in a suburban Boston parish caused a <u>significant</u>

upswing in the face of a diocese-wide downward trend. In the corporate world, that information would have set off bells and whistles at every level of the organization. Is Chancellor [name withheld] staff even aware of that account? You said absolutely nothing; one would think that seemingly remarkable phenomenon was never reported!

I also stated my belief that the hierarchy does not wish to deny pastors ready access to underposited collection funds, hence it's apparent aversion to secure Sunday collection procedures which, of necessity, deny even pastors ready access to those funds, you neither admitted nor contested that allegation, opting instead to ignore it altogether. As you know, however, silence in the face of such allegations is usually regarded as an admission.

I'll offer you just one more example, and this goes to the heart of the matter. I have repeatedly declared that the Church has no systems or procedures in effect to deter and/or detect theft of Sunday collection funds by clergy, employees or church members. I've also said that, absent secure collection, storage, counting and banking procedures, the only thefts that will ever surface are those discovered by accident or chance. I've likened them to the tip of an iceberg, and have even cited examples, most notably the North Providence parish plundered by its former pastor and an employee. You and other Church officials have never denied those claims, preferring instead to completely ignore them or allude to them as "alleged infractions" or in other equally vague jargon.

What really confounds me, Bishop Hughes, is that the hierarchy knows far better than I the incidence of discovered thefts, a figure which certainly surpasses the incidence of embezzlements receiving media coverage. You therefore know (or should know) that the Catholic Church is losing millions of dollars annually to theft from within. A good statistician can extrapolate known cases into an estimate of thefts than can reasonably be assumed to be ongoing at any given time. I have no doubt, on a national basis, that annual losses due to collection theft is in the tens, if not hundreds, of millions. Is it your position the hierarchy can defer action indefinitely, monumental ongoing losses aside, because it is unassertive or prefers (for whatever reason) not to exercise its administrative authority over pastors?

My father taught me the importance of supporting one's church. But he also taught me the value of a dollar. I support my own parish and feel good about it, because we have a <u>secure</u> Sunday collection system. I've concluded, however, that the hierarchy's apparent endorsement of substantial, ongoing theft relieves me of any obligation to support the CARDINAL'S APPEAL. Let's face it, what can my paltry $300 possibly mean to Archdiocesan stewards who feel free, <u>perhaps even obliged</u>, to shun the opportunity to generate anywhere from 1000 to 10,000 times that amount <u>annually</u>?

I must say, however, I was pleased to see that you acknowledge the hierarchy's role insofar as "stewardship of the funds of the faithful" is concerned. My entire argument springs from that premise. Unfortunately, that's also where we seem to part ways. I believe that, as stewards, the hierarchy bears a solemn duty to provide an adequate level of protection for the funds entrusted to them. For all practical purposes, that obligation <u>commences</u> when parishioners place their $5, $10 or $20 in the collection basket, not after the funds are deposited in the bank.

Individual pastors are <u>incapable</u> of developing and implementing the type of systems needed to establish true security over the Sunday collection. That's not a criticism, it's a simple fact! By refusing to develop and implement secure collection, storage counting and banking procedures, the Boston Archdiocese (not to mention other dioceses as well as the NCCB) is declaring that it is only concerned with the security of <u>deposited</u> funds. All the committees and meetings you can muster are and will remain merely pro forma actions, unless and until you confront and resolve the collection security issue. I'm far from the most confident man around, Bishop Hughes, but in this matter I <u>know</u> I'm right! How can anyone <u>credibly</u> hold that a <u>secure</u> Sunday collection system is unreasonable or undesirable?

I would appreciate your thoughtful consideration of the questions posed and statements made herein. If you detect any defects in the logic of my assertions Bishop Hughes, I would be pleased to learn the particulars. However, my special charge (as I see it) is to champion the fiscal wellbeing of the Faithful, few of whom are capable of fathoming the character and depth of this problem, let alone addressing it in a coherent fashion.

Nevertheless, it would sadden me, if you or any other members of the hierarchy in Boston or elsewhere mistook my fervor for personal animosity, as such is not the case.

You have my best wishes for every success in the fulfillment of your many challenging and sensitive responsibilities.

Most Sincerely,

Michael W. Ryan

[letterhead]

February 19, 1994

<u>PERSONAL AND CONFIDENTIAL</u>
Most Reverend Daniel W. Kucera, O.S.B.
Chairman, NCCB Committee on Budget & Finance
3060 Pennsylvania Avenue
Dubuque, IA 52001

Dear Archbishop Kucera:

From the standpoint of the fiscal wellbeing of the U.S. Catholic Church as well as the Archdiocese of Dubuque, this is the most important letter you will ever receive. Before I elaborate on that seemingly pompous claim, however, it would be helpful for you to know something of my background and motives.

I am a retired federal law enforcement official and a practicing Catholic. The agency I worked for is responsible for conducting financial audits and security surveys, in addition to enforcing a variety of federal criminal statutes. A summary of my education and professional career is enclosed.

Sometime prior to my retirement, I began to ponder the almost complete lack of security being afforded the Church's single most important source of revenue and object of my concern: the Sunday collection. My observations were based upon exposure to several parishes in as many states over 20+ years. At some point in my ruminations, it dawned on me that, in its 1900-year history, the Church has never implemented <u>effective</u> procedures to deter and/or detect Sunday collection embezzlements.

I became so intrigued that, shortly after retiring in December of 1986, I began efforts to make the hierarchy aware of the problem and available corrective measures. At this writing, however, my efforts have been an exercise in futility. At first, I operated under the assumption that failure to secure the Sunday collection system stemmed from a lack of knowledge and understanding about security concepts and the consequences that invariably follow a failure to apply them. Gradually, however, I've come to conclude that the problem goes much deeper than that. I am now convinced the hierarchy is aware of the problem but, for reasons best known to them, would rather countenance the loss of millions of dollars annually than confront and rectify the lack of adequate security.

The enclosed brochure presents a compelling case for protecting the Sunday collection. As you read the brochure, it is likely you'll wince at some of its more candid observations, especially those concerning the hierarchy's rejection of true security. No one enjoys being the object of criticism, least of all me, but history tells us that your predecessors <u>never</u> accepted the need for a secure collection system. They apparently preferred to look upon each theft incident as an anomaly that somehow did not exist before it was discovered, and could not be happening elsewhere because undiscovered embezzlements simply do not exist! If that strikes you as <u>Alice in Wonderland</u> thinking, you're right, but that, in effect, has been the hierarchy's posture to date.

What constitutes a secure Sunday collection system? Simply stated, it is one that <u>ensures</u> that every dollar placed in the collection basket on Saturday evening or Sunday morning is, <u>in fact</u>, deposited in the parish account. There is only one way to accomplish that objective: appropriate security equipment and procedures must be applied so that no one (not even the pastor) has lone, unobserved access to those funds from the time the collection is taken up, until all funds have been documented and deposited in the bank.

The "not even the pastor" caveat may seem unduly harsh but that is the nature of security. If the pastor has access, you can bet other people do also. And regardless of whether they do or they don't, pastors have also been known to succumb to the temptation presented by vulnerable Sunday collection funds. The hierarchy needs to look at security in the same light that police officers look at their firearms and body armor: it is <u>far</u> better to have those two items and not need them than it is to need them and not have them.

Regarding the incidence of embezzlement, consider the following. Because the Church has no system in place to deter and/or detect collection embezzlements, the only ones that will ever surface are those that are discovered by accident or chance. That being the case, what does surface can accurately be described as the proverbial "tip of the iceberg." Looking at it in another way, there are four basic levels of collection embezzlement awareness:

1.) thefts that are discovered and reported in the media;

2.) thefts that are discovered and brought to the attention of diocesan or archdiocesan officials but are withheld from the media;

3.) thefts that are discovered but are neither brought to the attention of diocesan officials nor the media; and

4.) thefts that are ongoing, having yet to be discovered.

I only have access to church embezzlement reports that appear in the few local newspapers I regularly read. In other words, my access to such information is limited to Level 1 cases, and is further greatly restricted by the scope of my reading as compared with the number of daily and weekly newspapers issued <u>nationally</u>. However, on that extremely limited basis alone, I can cite:

St. Anthony Church, Providence, RI - $200,000 for Pastor [name withheld] over the 3 years for which he was charged (That's $1,000+ per Sunday!);

St. Anthony Church, Providence, RI - $58,000 for another unnamed employee over the 2 years for which he was charged (That's $500+ per Sunday; they were thieving separately.)

Cathedral Santuario de Guadalupe, Dallas, TX - $240,000 for "a man trusted to count daily donations" over a six-year period ending in 1992 (That's $750+ per Sunday!);

St. Peter Claver Church, Simi Valley, CA - $60,000 for Father [name withheld] who also embezzled collection funds from his previous parish, Sacred Heart Church, Saticoy, CA; Father [name withheld] "always insisted on handling the collection money -- even at other priests' masses..."

St. Mary Magdalen Church, Waterbury, CT - $60,000 for a parishioner whose litany of service included Parish Council President, CCD Director, VP of the Catholic Women's Club, lector, fundraiser (ironically) and "Counter and depositor of the Sunday collection."

What will a secure Sunday collection system do for the American Catholic Church or the Archdiocese of Dubuque? Well, it probably won't keep some dioceses from going bankrupt as a result of the priest-pedophile lawsuits, but on a diocese-by-diocese basis it will increase annual revenue. In the Archdiocese of Dubuque (217 parishes?), for example, the figure could well be $500,000 or more annually. In my own parish, secure procedures are directly responsible for the recovery of at least $25,000 annually; $5,000 for the Christmas and Easter collections alone! You can confirm that with my pastor, Rev. [name withheld].

I'd like to conclude with a two-part rhetorical question, Archbishop Kucera, using the estimated cost of securing one parish's Sunday collection. The question is this: Would you invest $250 if you had good reason to believe it would be returned anywhere from 10 to 100 fold or more in one year? Assuming that return ($2,500 to $25,000 or more) was forthcoming, would you then invest $25 per year to ensure its annual continuance? I think you would readily agree that, for the average head of household, the answer to both questions would be a resounding "YES!" The question the NCCB Budget and Finance Committee should therefore address is this: Why do pastors (heads of parishes) and bishops (heads of dioceses) reply with a resounding "NO"?

My deep and abiding desire is to help ensure that the Catholic Church enters the 20th Century vis-a-vis collection security at least a few years before the rest of the world enters the 21st. I have the remedy but lack access to your inner circle. If your committee truly cares about the fiscal wellbeing of our Church, we can, quite literally, alter the course of history!

Most sincerely,

Michael W. Ryan

enclosures (4)

[letterhead]

May 5, 1994

<u>PERSONAL AND CONFIDENTIAL</u>
Most Reverend Thomas J. Murphy
Archbishop of Seattle
910 Marion Street
Seattle, WA 98104

Dear Archbishop Murphy:

I am writing in regard to Archbishop Kucera's March 1 letter acknowledging my earlier correspondence and relating its referral to you, his successor as Chairman of the NCCB Committee on Budget and Finance. I have not heard from you, and am therefore taking the liberty of providing you with a copy of the file to cover the possibility that Archbishop Kucera's referral went astray. I do hope you will share it with the other members of your committee.

I read of the Holy Father's upcoming convocation to consider how the Church can best prepare itself for the Third Millennium. Assuming this meeting will cover both the secular and spiritual realms, I would like to respectfully call to your attention the manifest need for an adequate level of security over the Church's single most important source of revenue: the Sunday collection.

I recently prepared the enclosed brochure as an adjunct to my ongoing efforts to make the hierarchy not only aware of this issue but interested enough to explore its various ramifications. What better way to fiscally prepare our Church for the Third Millennium than to insure the safety and integrity of the Sunday collection, our main source of revenue?

Frankly, Archbishop Murphy, I'm dumbfounded at the Church's seeming unwillingness to brush aside the cobwebs of tradition and territorialism, thereby exposing the folly of a vulnerable Sunday collection system. As the Budget and Finance Committee chairman, you are in a unique position to influence the hierarchy on this critical issue. There is no greater service you can perform for the fiscal wellbeing of our

Church than to embrace and champion the adoption of genuinely secure procedures for protecting the Sunday collection. The prelate who recognizes and acts upon that simple truth will be revered for generations to come!

Most sincerely,

Michael W. Ryan

enclosures (4)

[letterhead]

November 3, 1994

<u>PERSONAL AND CONFIDENTIAL</u>
William Cardinal Keeler, D.D. J.C.D.
Archbishop of Baltimore
President, N.C.C.B.
320 Cathedral Street
Baltimore, MD 21201

Dear Cardinal Keeler:

I am writing to you in regard to a matter of vital importance to the moral and fiscal wellbeing of the U. S. Catholic Church.

Before I elaborate, however, I ask that you picture yourself as being in a position of authority similar to the one you presently occupy, but it is the 1950's or 1960's. One day, you receive a letter from a reputable Catholic psychologist or psychiatrist who states that he's uncovered a psychological condition which he believes is more prevalent among Catholic priests than anyone has yet imagined. He goes on to state it is highly probable the few cases he is aware of (you are aware of others) are only the proverbial "tip of the iceberg." He further states that the cases he knows of were mishandled (the priests involved were merely transferred) and he concludes with the opinion that this psychological condition, pedophilia, will not go away on its own, but rather will require in–depth study, testing and intense, long–term treatment previously unheard of within the Catholic Church.

I don't know if something along those lines occurred back then but, if it did, that concerned Catholic professional was either totally ignored or (more likely) given the brush–off, i.e., "Thank you for your concern. I am referring your letter to (whoever) as information and for any follow–up deemed warranted..." or words to that effect. Whether it did or didn't occur, we know the Church didn't give the priest–pedophile problem <u>proactive</u> attention until the media gave it intense, widespread coverage. You know better that I what that postponement cost the Church in terms of moral degradation as well as financial settlements and damaged credibility.

The condition I now bring to your attention, Cardinal Keeler, is embezzlement from the Sunday collection, the Church's single most important source of revenue. As you know, the Church has no effective system in place to either deter or detect surreptitious thefts from the Sunday collection. As a retired criminal investigator (see enclosed resume), I can assure you the absence of <u>effective</u> security measures virtually guarantees that repetitive embezzlements will occur and, in an organization of this size, the cases that come to the surface are merely the tip of the previously referenced iceberg. I am enclosing summaries of a few such cases, as information. Undoubtedly, you have access to others that did not reach the media.

Before security over any Sunday collection can be deemed adequate, appropriate security equipment and procedures must be applied so that no one – <u>not even the pastor</u> – has lone, unobserved access to those funds or any portion thereof <u>at any time</u>. This embargo must begin immediately after the collection is taken up (when it is consolidated at the rear of the church) and must remain intact and absolutely unbroken until the collection has been processed and properly deposited in the bank. As you know, the Church does not even come close to meeting that criteria!

In addition to losing tens of millions of dollars annually, you must recognize that we are talking about a moral evil – temptation to sin – which is well within your power and that of your brother Bishops to eliminate or at least <u>greatly</u> reduce. I happen to have the cure for this problem, but the really important issue is whether anyone in authority is even willing to admit that the problem exists. Seven years of brush-offs tell me they're not, and I'm now at your doorstep to see if you will be the one who finally confronts the reality of this evil and takes positive action.

I'm sure some of the fears that kept your predecessors from confronting the priest-pedophile tragedy are present in this situation. Obviously, an unknown number of pastors and priests supplement their income from undeposited Sunday collection funds. Certainly, many previously undiscovered embezzlements will surface with implementation of secure procedures; some of them will reach the media, much to your/our embarrassment. And a number of parish volunteers will be insulted by the implications of security – the embezzlers will be especially vociferous. But in spite of the "negatives", it should be as clear to you as it is to me, Cardinal Keeler, that the cure is in no way, shape or form worse than the disease!

I'm convinced the phenomenon of Sunday collection embezzlement is pandemic. You may believe it is something less than that, but the point is: we both know it exists and will continue to exist unless and until someone like yourself subjugates his organizational pride, girds himself and takes positive action. I stand ready to assist, but the "ball" is in your court. I pray that God will grant you the wisdom to see what must be done and the courage to do it. Toward that end, I conclude with the words of St. Pius X on the occasion of the beatification of St. Joan of Arc.

> *"In our time more than ever before*
> *the greatest asset of the evilly disposed*
> *is the cowardice and weakness of good men,*
> *and all the vigor of Satan's reign*
> *is due to the easygoing weakness of Catholics."*

Most sincerely,

Michael W. Ryan

[letterhead]

November 13, 1994

<u>PERSONAL AND CONFIDENTIAL</u>
Most Reverend Thomas J. Murphy
Archbishop of Seattle
Chairman, NCCB Committee on Budget & Finance
910 Marion Street
Seattle, WA 98104

Dear Archbishop Murphy:

I have an embarrassing confession to make. When I wrote you on May 5 in follow-up to my letter to Archbishop Kucera, former Chairman of the NCCB Budget and Finance Committee, I failed to recognize I had written you in 1992 when you were Chairman of the Committee on Stewardship. However, you apparently remembered our correspondence and concluded it was time to simply ignore me. After seven years of fruitless contact with the hierarchy, I've become accustomed to eliciting that sort of response. Nevertheless, I'm still at the keyboard and my enthusiasm for the challenge remains unchanged.

In your January 11, 1993 letter, you stated the issue of security over the Sunday collection was outside the responsibility of the NCCB Committee on Stewardship, and suggested that I contact the Diocesan Fiscal Officers organization. I did so and was accorded the expected treatment: Rev. [name withheld] did not deem my letter worthy of acknowledgment.

I mention this, because I want to be sure you understand I've followed every conceivable lead in my ongoing efforts to "reach" the appropriate officials.

Now, you head the <u>Committee on Budget and Finance</u>, and I am writing you about ongoing <u>theft</u> from the Church's largest source of <u>revenue</u>. Most people I know would conclude I'm in the right pew as well as the right church, yet you completely disregarded my May 5 letter. As I advised you on November 30, 1992, the matter of Sunday collection embezzlement is as old as the Church itself and occurs <u>weekly</u> in an unknown but significant number of parishes <u>nationwide</u>. You know that at least as well as I do, Archbishop Murphy, even though you're loath to admit it to an "outsider" like me.

Whoever said those who forget the mistakes of history are bound to repeat them, could well have been talking about the Church. The ongoing priest-pedophile calamity first surfaced in the 1960s or earlier but was not <u>proactively</u> addressed by you and/or your predecessors until 25-30 years later - and then only because of <u>intense</u> media coverage. Having been on the receiving end of seven years of dissembling, it's clear to me that you and your brother bishops have, for reasons best known to yourselves, decided a secure Sunday collection is not in <u>your</u> best interests. Surely, no one can <u>honestly</u> claim security is not in the flock's best interests! Whatever your reasons for rejecting collection security, none can or ever will be legitimate.

The Marine Corps is known for its emphasis on "a few good men." The Church only needs one well-placed member of the hierarchy to reverse <u>centuries</u> of neglect. The time to end all the buck-passing, to drop all the defenses and pretense, is long gone. It is within your grasp to be the prelate who first recognized Satan's hand in a <u>highly</u> vulnerable Sunday collection <u>and</u> who then took positive action to eradicate it. I pray that God will grant you the wisdom to recognize that simple truth, Archbishop Murphy, and the courage to respond objectively. Toward that end, I offer the words of St. Pius X, given on the occasion of the beatification of St. Joan of Arc.

> *"In our time more than ever before*
> *the greatest asset of the evilly disposed*
> *is the cowardice and weakness of good men,*
> *and all the vigor of Satan's reign*
> *is due to the easygoing weakness of Catholics."*

I don't pretend to be familiar with the character of St. Pius X, but he is, after all, a Saint, and the Most Reverend Jan Olav Smit apparently thought enough of him to author his biography which the Daughters of St. Paul (*HEAVENLY FRIENDS, a saint for each day*) describe as a "Journey through the boyhood, priesthood, papacy and sainthood of this remarkable man - warm, loving, humorous - capable of leading the people of God with extraordinary wisdom - the influence of which we still feel in the Church today."

St. Pius X certainly sounds like a man who was far more concerned with leaving his mark than he was with marking time.
It seems clear he did not subscribe to the "go along, to get
along" philosophy which permeates many of the bureaucratic
structures in today's society. I don't doubt for a minute that
you have had a number of defining moments in your life and
vocation, Archbishop Murphy, and that you responded in the
finest Christian tradition. But this is a once-in-a-lifetime
challenge to reshape and secure the fiscal lifeline of the
Church, the same lifeline that has formed the basis for a
number of church closings in recent years. Yet, strangely, no
one is willing to even recognize, let alone examine or discuss
the matter. Isn't it high time someone did?

I stand ready to assist you in this formidable undertaking,
Archbishop Murphy, but only you can take the first positive
step toward its completion. I look forward to receiving your
reply.

Most sincerely,

Michael W. Ryan

[letterhead]

March 9, 1995

<u>PERSONAL AND CONFIDENTIAL</u>
Most Reverend Thomas J. Murphy
Archbishop of Seattle
Chairman, NCCB Committee on Budget & Finance
910 Marion Street
Seattle, WA 98104

Dear Archbishop Murphy:

This refers to my letter of November 13, 1994 concerning the nationwide dearth of security for Sunday collection funds. While I do not doubt that you received that letter as well as prior unacknowledged correspondence, I am enclosing a copy for your convenience.

Frankly, Archbishop Murphy, I can see why many victims of priest-inflicted abuse are so bitter and frequently found it necessary to bring suit against the Church just to obtain reasonable reparations. The hierarchy has raised stonewalling to the status of an art form. One cannot help wondering exactly when Jesus' admonition to "be the servant of all" was jettisoned by your predecessors. Regardless, I remain committed to the cause of convincing you and your brother bishops of the absolute need to implement genuinely secure collection, storage, counting and banking procedures <u>nationwide</u>.

It is not inappropriate to remind ourselves that the money parishioners place in the collection basket each Sunday is given in the belief that it will be protected from seizure and conversion by persons (pastors included) who, in the absence of adequate <u>internal</u> security, are able to <u>repeatedly</u> embezzle such funds without notice or detection. While I'm sure you would not disagree with that representation, neither you nor any other prelate I know of can correctly give that assurance under the present conditions.

As Chairman of the NCCB Budget and Finance Committee, I assume that you have personal expertise in this area and/or have one or more financial experts on or available to your committee. With that in mind, I would like to offer what I consider incontrovertible proof of the point I have been trying to make for the past several years, i.e., that the U.S. Catholic Church has been and is now remiss in its obligation to protect its greatest source of revenue: the Sunday collection.

The source for the "proof" I now offer is a November 1972 publication issued by the American Institute of Certified Public Accountants (AICPA). It is entitled "Statement on Auditing Standards - Codification of Auditing Standards and Procedures." Selected sections of the AICPA statement will be contrasted with the Church's current and historical posture concerning the Sunday collection. I hope you will bear with me on this.

Section 320 of the AICPA standards concerns the study and evaluation of internal control; Section 320.42 states, in pertinent part:

> "The objective of safeguarding assets requires that access be limited to authorized personnel. The number and caliber of personnel to whom access is authorized should be influenced by the nature of the assets and the related susceptibility to loss through errors and irregularities. Limitation of direct access to assets requires appropriate physical segregation and protective equipment or devices." (emphasis added)

The terms "errors" and "irregularities" are applied to differentiate between accidental and intentional wrongdoing. When one considers "the nature of the assets" we're dealing with (significant amounts of undocumented currency) their "related susceptibility to loss" should be obvious. Yet the need for "appropriate physical segregation and protective equipment" is presently and has historically been left to the discretion of pastors who know little or nothing about internal control, especially as it relates to cash receipts.

Section 320.44 of the AICPA standards states, in pertinent part:

> ". . . agreement of a cash count with the recorded balance does not provide evidence that all cash received has been properly recorded. This illustrates an unavoidable distinction between fiduciary and recorded accountability: the former arises immediately upon acquisition of an

asset; the latter arises only when the initial record of the transaction is prepared." (emphasis added)

In the case of the Sunday collection, I trust you would agree that, for the Church, fiduciary accountability begins when a parishioner places his or her offering in the collection basket. Under present procedures, however, the number of people (clergy, staff and volunteers) having lone, unobserved access to the collection or any portion thereof every week in a typical parish, prior to its tabulation and deposit (recorded accountability), would leave even the "greenest" of auditors aghast.

Insofar as the evaluation of any control system is concerned, Section 320.65 of the AICPA standards states, in pertinent part:

". . . apply the following steps in considering each significant class of transactions and related assets involved in the audit:

a. Consider the types of errors and irregularities that could occur.

b. Determine the accounting control procedures that should prevent or detect such errors and irregularities.

c. Determine whether necessary procedures are prescribed and are being followed satisfactorily."

I respectfully suggest that if the Sunday collection system had ever been examined in that manner and an appropriate report had been submitted and had been effectively acted upon, my efforts over the past several years would have been unnecessary.

I will conclude these citations, Archbishop Murphy, with the opening sentence of Section 110.02 of the AICPA standards:

"Management has the responsibility for adopting sound accounting policies, for maintaining an adequate and effective system of accounts, for the safeguarding of assets, and for devising a system of internal control that will, among other things, help assure the production of proper financial statements." (emphasis added)

With all due respect, it seems apparent that neither you nor any other member of the hierarchy, present or past, has fulfilled that responsibility, insofar as it relates to our single most important source of revenue: the Sunday collection. It is not enough for you and your brother bishops to be <u>aware</u> of your fiduciary responsibilities; that is only a beginning and means little, if it is not accompanied by <u>positive action</u> which establishes a level of security sufficient to guarantee strict control and accountability.

Finally, Archbishop Murphy, I respectfully suggest the NCCB undertake a definitive test within a designated diocese or archdiocese to resolve the obvious divergence of opinion that presently exists with respect to the integrity of our Sunday collection system. A sample of parishes within the designated diocese/archdiocese (5 - 10%) should provide a sufficient basis for extrapolating the results. For implementation and monitoring purposes, it would be prudent to focus on a particular geographic area of the diocese/archdiocese. But within that area, a mix of urban, suburban and rural parishes should be selected, to ensure that the test parishes reflect an accurate cross section of the diocese/archdiocese as a whole.

As you might recall from earlier correspondence, I developed a system for protecting Sunday collection funds between basket and bank and all points between. It has been proven and I would be pleased to permit its use (at no cost) in connection with the above described test program. It is important to note, however, the test period would have to span a year or more, to ensure the accumulation of sufficient data upon which the program coordinators' conclusions and recommendations can be based. I project that at least 20% of the parishes involved in the test will experience a <u>substantial</u> increase in <u>cash</u> receipts as a direct result of the security measures. I'm also convinced the cost of conducting the test will be more than offset by the increased revenue.

One final note: Believe it or not, I'm more of a doer than a dissenter, and would be willing to assist in organizing and conducting any such test program. Please do not hesitate to contact me, Archbishop Murphy, if you need additional information or wish to discuss any aspect of my proposal. In any event, I would greatly appreciate the courtesy of a reply.

Most Sincerely,

Michael W. Ryan

enclosure

[letterhead]

March 23, 1995

<u>PERSONAL AND CONFIDENTIAL</u>
William Cardinal Keeler, President
National Conference of Catholic Bishops
3211 4th Street N.E.
Washington, DC 20017-1194

Dear Cardinal Keeler:

This refers to my letter of November 3, 1994 concerning the fiscal and moral wellbeing of the U. S. Catholic Church. A copy of that unacknowledged letter is enclosed as information. Also enclosed is a copy of my most recent letter (3-9-95) to Archbishop Thomas J. Murphy, Chairman of the Committee on Budget and Finance. As Archbishop Murphy's "superior" within the NCCB, I feel it is particularly appropriate for you to be aware of its contents.

In my letter to Archbishop Murphy, I cited certain basic tenets of the American Institute of Certified Public Accountants concerning internal control and the safeguarding of assets. In spite of their universal relevance, the Church (in the person of its hierarchy) has somehow rationalized that they are not applicable. From a fiscal standpoint, that posture is completely indefensible, and the moral ramifications of deliberately maintaining a vulnerable Sunday collection system are scandalous. I have cited a number of Biblical passages in past correspondence, including JOHN 12.6, LUKE 17.1 and MARK 9.35, which <u>directly</u> relate to this issue. While they have been fruitless, I would like to suggest MATTHEW 21.13 for your contemplation. I believe it applies as much today as it did when Jesus drove the merchants from the Temple. Today, He would say: "...you are *keeping* it a hideout for thieves!"

I am well aware of the Church's unique structure, Cardinal Keeler. That is why I put the word *superior* in quotes. Uniqueness notwithstanding, however, each and every organization that acquires assets has a fiduciary responsibility to protect those assets. Intentional failure to protect such assets is commonly termed *nonfeasance.* Quite frankly, I cannot conceive of any mitigating circumstance that would except the hierarchy from that negative classification. Indeed, the highly vulnerable nature of Sunday collection funds only renders the hierarchy's failure to protect it all the more egregious.

Like most prelates, you undoubtedly have a "full plate." I'm sure you'd like nothing better than for me to find another cause (unrelated to my Church) so that I might cease nettling you and your brother bishops on this matter. *"Surely,"* you might be thinking, *"the Church has survived for nearly 2000 years without securing the Sunday collection; why is it suddenly so important to take corrective action now, in this decade, during my tenure?"* The answer, of course, is that the need has always existed. The failure of your predecessors to take needed corrective action in no way diminishes your obligation to take appropriate action at this time. In fact, the availability of modern security concepts and methods that were not available to your predecessors only serves to strengthen your obligation to act while, at the same time, intensifying the civil and moral consequences of your failure to act. Can you name even one business or organization (excluding the Church) that is poised to enter the 21st Century with 19th Century cash processing methods still firmly in place?

As I have indicated in prior correspondence, Cardinal Keeler, I'm a team player. Presently, however, you and I are on opposing teams. My team is playing to secure an economic win for the Church. Your team, I'm sorry to say, is playing to keep the Church mired in theft, fiscal jeopardy and moral decay. If that isn't a classic *Alice in Wonderland* scenario, I don't know what is. In all my 58 years, I have never felt more in the right, and each disingenuous and/or vacuous reply I receive from a member of the hierarchy (when they deign to respond) only serves to confirm that feeling. It seems as though you've reasoned (as a group) that an objectively imprudent, immoral and (quite possibly) unlawful omission can be deemed wise, moral and lawful if knowledge of its existence is restricted to the clique that perpetuates it. Are sins of omission no longer among the Church's list of moral wrongs?

We've all been desensitized to some degree or other by society's many allurements, but I'd like to believe you haven't lost your ability to ponder an important issue and make a clear, accurate assessment, at least insofar as the moral/theological aspects are concerned. Clearly, the NCCB doesn't seem to have any difficulty fathoming the intricacies of state and federal legislation impacting our society. Why has it been so difficult for you to even recognize the problems inherent in our historically vulnerable Sunday collection? The only conclusion an informed observer can reach is that the NCCB, as a group, and the bishops, as the heads of their respective dioceses, are deliberately stonewalling to maintain the status quo. Certainly, if anything was learned from the priest/pedophile debacle, it is that dissembling and stonewalling only serve to make matters worse - morally, fiscally and psychologically.

I can't promise you that implementation of secure collection, storage, counting and banking procedures will be absolutely painless. There will be "problems" in getting from where we are (vulnerable and hemorrhaging) to where we need to be (secure and fiscally sound). But not one of those problems will have any validity, and all of them can and will be conquered. To paraphrase an old saying, *"right makes might"* and this crusade is as right as any can be. As the official representative of the Catholic Bishops of the United States, Cardinal Keeler, you have a special obligation not to ignore or brush aside this call for long-delayed justice. I pray that our Lord will inspire, strengthen and guide you in rectifying this critical matter.

Most sincerely,

Michael W. Ryan

enclosures (3)

[letterhead]

January 1, 1996

<u>PERSONAL AND CONFIDENTIAL</u>
Most Reverend Anthony M. Pilla, D.D., M.A.
Bishop of Cleveland
1027 Superior Avenue
Cleveland, OH 44114

Dear Bishop Pilla:

I am writing to you as a practicing Catholic and retired federal law enforcement official who has spent much of the past several years exploring the problem of church embezzlement, particularly as it relates to the historically vulnerable Sunday collection. As such, I look upon myself as one of many lay people who have been *out of the pews* for quite some time. Among those who know me, some might even say my knowledge and insight relating to collection security qualify me for association with what the NCCB recently identified as the *wisdom of the laity*. A brief résumé of my professional experience is enclosed.

As you must know, Bishop Pilla, the hierarchy has never addressed comprehensively the ongoing issue and incidence of embezzlement from the Sunday collection. The enclosed news summary highlights only a few of those cases reaching media attention over the past several years. In addition, it seems clear that many cases involving morally errant priests involve misuse of church monies, including Sunday collection funds which are typically not protected against internal theft. Examples include the infamous Fr. [name withheld] and Msgr. [name withheld] of San Francisco, and Fr. [name withheld] of Washington, DC. These and other cases you surely know of clearly establish that no one, by virtue of their status or position, is immune to the temptation presented by a vulnerable Sunday collection.

For several years now, I have sought to make that simple point with various NCCB officials. I have been singularly unsuccessful, however, and it strikes me as highly strange (to say the least) that the NCCB can comprehend and divine complex national and international issues over which they have <u>no</u> control - issuing elaborate pronouncements detailing what can and should be done - while at the same time turning a blind eye to a patently economic <u>and</u> moral evil over which it has <u>complete</u> control. I cannot help but equate that disparity with Jesus' query: *"Why do you look at the speck in your brother's eye, but pay no attention to the log in your own eye?"* Make no mistake about it, Bishop Pilla, the NCCB's ongoing and apparently deliberate shunning of the collection security issue is a very large *log*, one which is costing the U. S. Catholic Church tens if not hundreds of millions of dollars <u>annually</u>!

As I advised at least two of your predecessors, Bishop Pilla, I stand ready to assist the NCCB in addressing and resolving this most disgraceful situation. I am well aware of the stumbling blocks, all but one of which begin with the words *fear of,* and none of which are in any way legitimate. The stumbling block that doesn't begin with those words involves sovereignty, i.e., the autonomy of individual bishops, archbishops and cardinals. In this case, however, such autonomy can only be viewed as an excuse to avoid addressing what any person who takes the time to give it diligent thought knows is and has for many years been a neglected, <u>Church-wide</u> moral and economic imperative.

I can imagine you're wondering what P.S. SERVICES is and where it fits into this matter. The name was coined and registered by me in late 1986 when I began to think about what I would do in my retirement; I had the intention of becoming a freelance Security Consultant. That aspiration was short lived, however, and I soon found myself using the name primarily as a vehicle for making contacts. In all the years since the inception of P.S. SERVICES, I have garnered <u>not one penny</u> of income from or as a result of it.

Finally, Bishop Pilla, I hope you will forgive the bluntness (you might even say, irreverence) of my approach, but I long ago dispensed with the customary protocols, to more effectively advance what I perceive to be the unvarnished truth relating to this issue. The only question that matters is whether the issue I have unearthed is important - I believe it is critically so - and warrants the collective attention of your organization. Again, I stand ready to assist the NCCB in any way it will permit me, in order to ensure that our Church does not enter the 21st

Century still clinging to woefully deficient, economically debilitating, sin-proliferating, 19th Century methods and procedures.

Most Sincerely,

Michael W. Ryan

[letterhead]

March 24, 1996

<u>PERSONAL AND CONFIDENTIAL</u>
Most Reverend Anthony M. Pilla, D.D., M.A.
Bishop of Cleveland
1027 Superior Avenue
Cleveland, OH 44114

Dear Bishop Pilla:

Enclosed is a copy of a letter I directed to [name withheld], Associate General Secretary of the NCCB/USCC. As you will note, it concerns my letter to you of January 1 regarding the Church-wide lack of adequate security for Sunday collection funds.

As I have advised other members of the hierarchy, Bishop Pilla, I am committed to the pursuit of this issue for as long as it takes for someone of your stature and office to recognize the folly of continued inaction and move to rectify this dishonorable and immoral situation. That can only happen through Church-wide dissemination and implementation of concrete security measures that will both deter and detect embezzlements from the Sunday collection. I advise you of my commitment not convey a *threat* but rather to make clear to you the enduring nature of my commitment to the fiscal well–being of our Church.

If my persistence causes you to take a fresh, objective look at this issue, free of any antagonism or previously formed judgments that might have been passed along to you by one or more of my prior correspondents, I will be greatly heartened; I don't see how anyone could examine the matter objectively and conclude that prompt corrective action is unwarranted.

Once again, Bishop Pilla, let me assure you of my availability and willingness to assist the NCCB in any way it will permit me to help ensure that our Church does not enter the 21th Century still clinging to grossly deficient 19th Century procedures.

Most Sincerely,

Michael W. Ryan

[letterhead]

January 22, 1997

<u>PERSONAL AND CONFIDENTIAL</u>
Most Reverend Anthony M. Pilla, D.D., M.A.
President, National Conference of Catholic Bishops
3211 Fourth Street
Washington, DC 20017-1194

Dear Bishop Pilla:

This refers to my letters of January 1 and March 24, 1996 regarding the Church–wide lack of adequate security for Sunday collection funds.

As you know, I corresponded with NCCB/USCC Associate General Secretary [name withheld] who responded on your behalf to my January 1 letter. Not having received any reply to my March 24 letters, I sent a follow-up to [name withheld] on August 28. I can't recall sending you a copy of that follow-up and am therefore taking the liberty of furnishing one at this time.

As you will note, I included in the August 28 letter a syllogism that came to mind one day while I was pondering the issue. That syllogism imposes upon the hierarchy ultimate responsibility for <u>most</u> Sunday collection embezzlements. I'm certainly no theologian but, having gotten no correction from [name withheld], I feel safe in assuming the syllogism is sound. In any event, I recently began to think about the ramifications of that syllogism and, in the process, came up with another syllogism which, if true, places an even greater moral obligation on the hierarchy. That syllogism reads as follows:

> Major Premise:
> Embezzlement [the unauthorized, surreptitious removal/misappropriation of funds] from the Sunday collection - whether committed by a pastor, priest, employee or volunteer - is a sin.

> Minor Premise:
> <u>Most</u> Sunday collection embezzlements <u>and their concomitant sins</u> can be prevented by simple, inexpensive

security measures the U. S. Catholic hierarchy is well aware of but refuses to employ.

Conclusion:
The U. S. Catholic hierarchy bears <u>ultimate</u> responsibility for the sins that flow from <u>most</u> Sunday collection embezzlements.

Quite frankly, Bishop Pilla, I'm not as confident about the accuracy of this syllogism as I was about the first. I would therefore appreciate receiving your opinion as to its accuracy and, if you deem it faulty, the identity of the incorrect premise or conclusion. Naturally, if you discover an error in the first syllogism, I would certainly appreciate being advised of the particulars so that I might adjust my thinking on this critical issue.

If I'm correct, however, you and the USCC/NCCB membership have a crucial decision to make. You must ask yourselves this question: *Having been shown the light, do we nevertheless continue to be the ultimate cause of most Sunday collection thefts and the sins they represent, or do we put aside the petty, elitist resentment we so obviously hold for the messenger, swallow our pride and do what clearly needs to be done?* Every time I think about this shameful situation, I am absolutely dumbfounded that our Lord has allowed such an evil scenario to be played out for so long without divine intervention. But then I remember that, in His eyes, we're all the same; crosiers and miters notwithstanding, we'll all be judged on the basis of the good and evil we did and, I believe, on the good we should have done but knowingly failed to do.

Lord knows, Bishop Pilla, I'll have plenty to answer for, but I don't believe my attempts to goad the hierarchy into fulfilling their fiduciary responsibility and eliminating occasions of sin will be part of it. It would be disingenuous of me to imply that I'm pursuing this matter because I'm worried about the souls of the hierarchy. I have enough to worry about within the circle of my family and friends. I can't help thinking, however, that if you and your brother bishops have absolutely nothing but this perennial case of willful evasion to answer for, Jesus' admonition to his disciples in Luke 17.1 should give all of you ample cause for concern.

*"Things that make people fall into sin are bound to happen,
but how terrible for the one who makes them happen!"*

I would like very much to hear from you, Bishop Pilla. What I'm offering the hierarchy comes under the heading of *Gifts of the Laity*. You really should take advantage of it.

Most Sincerely,

M. W. Ryan

[letterhead]

March 4, 1997

<u>PERSONAL AND CONFIDENTIAL</u>
Most Reverend Anthony M. Pilla, President
National Conference of Catholic Bishops
3211 Fourth Street N.E
Washington, DC 20017-1194

Dear Bishop Pilla:

Thank you for replying to my letter of January 22 which concerned the moral implications of the U. S. Bishops' ongoing and willful failure to adequately protect Sunday collection funds.

In your letter, you allude to [the Associate General Secretary's] acknowledgment of my January 1, 1996 letter to you regarding this same topic. You mention the Accounting Practices Committee of the USCC as having *"proposed means for bishops to develop better internal financial controls at the diocesan level."* You further state you are *"confident that the bishops of this country are aware of this issue* [the evil of fraud and embezzlement] *and that they take appropriate measures in their dioceses to safeguard against it."*

I certainly agree the bishops are aware of the issue, but I've seen nothing to suggest that any of them have taken appropriate measures to safeguard against the ongoing phenomenon of Sunday collection embezzlement. Indeed, the USCC's own Committee on Budget and Finance seems to have made a special effort to omit from its recent guideline <u>Diocesan Internal Controls, A Framework</u> any *"appropriate measures"* for protecting Sunday collection funds. I noted that glaring omission in my March 24, 1996 letter to [the Associate General Secretary], a copy of which was referred to you contemporaneously.

With all due respect, Bishop Pilla, I must conclude with one final observation concerning you and all of your predecessors and peers with whom I have corresponded over nearly 10 years. Not one of you has ever acknowledged or attempted to refute the negative moral ramifications of your ongoing failure to curtail the perennial evil of Sunday collection theft! Isn't it high time you and your brother bishops complied with the Scriptures' various highly pertinent admonitions? Until you do take appropriate action, your claim to moral leadership will remain deeply flawed.

Most sincerely,

Michael W. Ryan

[letterhead]

November 28, 1999

<u>PERSONAL ATTENTION</u>
Most Reverend Joseph Fiorenza, President
National Conference of Catholic Bishops
3211 Fourth Street N.E
Washington, DC 20017-1194

Dear Bishop Fiorenza:

Inasmuch as the NCCB and its members are the subject of the enclosed brochure, I felt it appropriate that you be furnished a copy.

You have probably never heard of me or my ten-year quest to cause the NCCB to respond to the fact that the Church's fiscal integrity demands that they, <u>as a group</u>, proactively address the critical issue of security over its principal source of revenue, the Sunday collection. To save you time and wasted effort, be advised that I have heard the standard explanation from Bishop Pilarczyk, Cardinal Keeler and Bishop Pilla, among others, and know the NCCB's official position is that it cannot mandate the manner in which collection funds are handled within individual dioceses, that responsibility resting solely with the individual bishops. With all due respect, however, I cannot accept that excuse. Individual bishops also possess authority over Catholic universities and colleges within their dioceses, but that did not keep the Conference from recently agreeing upon the all-encompassing standards and requirements of *Ex Corde Ecclesiae*.

I will also save you the trouble of citing the NCCB's issuance of Publication #5-056 as evidence of its good faith in the matter of collection security. As you will note from my letter of March 24, 1996 to [name withheld], copy herewith, I see it as exactly the opposite; the dearth of information on how collection funds should be safeguarded actually evidences the Conference's bad faith.

The following paragraph constitutes that Publication 5-056's sole reference to Sunday collection funds.

[Author's note: As the subject publication is copyrighted and I sincerely doubt the USCCB would knowingly authorize the appearance of any portion of it in this book, it has been excised from this letter which, in all other respects, is a verbatim transcript. Suffice it to say, my earlier assessment stands: "its coverage of the Sunday collection consists of one very short paragraph entitled 'Handling of Collections' that contains so little guidance it is virtually useless. Indeed, some of what little was said could well help to mask and perpetuate ongoing thefts."]

From that narrative, a person might conclude that collection thefts only occur during the counting process. The referenced publication is devoid of the kind of detail essential to the development of a <u>genuinely</u> secure Sunday collection system. There is nothing in that slap-dab treatment of a church's principal source of revenue that would keep a collector, pastor, associate, housekeeper or other opportunist from invading the collection sacks/baskets for loose currency prior to the counting process. Consider this, Bishop Fiorenza: <u>a single column of the enclosed brochure (1/3 page) contains far more detail on how collection funds must be protected than do all 22 pages comprising Publication #5-056</u>! It's absolutely mind boggling!

Of course, Bishop T. J. Murphy would quickly direct our attention to the Foreword which includes the following note: *"The document addresses concerns at a diocesan level and does not specifically deal with issues at a parish or other institutional level."* That would seem to be a valid *escape clause* were it not for the fact that the publication gives detailed treatment to other parish-level financial activities, including control of assets and accounting records, bank accounts, <u>cash</u> disbursements, petty <u>cash</u>, <u>cash</u> receipts, receivables, payables and purchase orders. Clearly, someone made a conscious decision to exclude any meaningful guidelines and directives relating to the protection of Sunday collection funds. It's a <u>nationwide</u> problem involving our <u>principal</u> source of revenue! Obviously, it should be dealt with at the <u>national</u> level.

I am encouraged, Bishop Fiorenza, by your Nov. 15 statement regarding the courage of your predecessors: *"They faced the significant issues of their times"* and your acknowledgment that the current membership *"must face the issues that will come our way in the future."* It gives me hope that you will not disregard or downplay the tragic cases of [name withheld], [name withheld] (TX), Rev. [name withheld] and [name withheld] (RI) [name withheld] (CT) Rev. [name withheld] (CA) and all the Sunday collection thieves we both know are presently practicing their weekly *business* with great ease, compliments of the NCCB. My fondest hope, is that you will recognize them for what they are (symptoms of an inherent but very curable weakness) and do what we both know must be done.

A few years ago, while pondering causes and effects, a syllogism came into my mind; I would very much like to shelve it as being no longer applicable. It reads as follows:

Major Premise: The proximate cause of all Sunday collection embezzlements is the moral weakness of those individuals who commit such embezzlements.

Minor Premise: Most Sunday collection embezzlements can be prevented by simple, inexpensive security measures the hierarchy is well aware of but refuses to employ.

Conclusion: The ultimate cause of most Sunday collection embezzlements is the hierarchy's willful rejection of simple, inexpensive and readily available security measures.

If that syllogism withstands your theological scrutiny, Bishop Fiorenza, and we can agree embezzlement is sinful, a companion syllogism arises. If I were a bishop, I would find the ramifications of that syllogism very disconcerting and, as President of the Conference, I would feel morally obliged to do everything in my power to correct it. I pray that you and your brother bishops will promptly acknowledge and aggressively fulfill that moral obligation.

I look forward to hearing from you and, as always, I stand ready to assist in any way possible.

Most sincerely,

Michael W. Ryan

[NCCB Logo]

Office of the General Secretary

3211 Fourth Street NE Washington DC 20017-1194
Most Reverend Joseph A. Fiorenza, D.D.
Bishop of Galveston-Houston
President

December 7, 1999

Dear Mr. Ryan:

I want to acknowledge your letter of November 28, 1999 to Bishop Joseph Fiorenza as President of the National Conference of Catholic Bishops. While you requested that it receive his "personal attention", it has been referred to me for a response because of my extensive experience in dealing with the issues you raise.

I understand the major point of your letter and the enclosed pamphlet from P.S. Services to be that there should be some national teaching position, policy or procedure developed to prevent embezzlement in local parishes. You are correct that "the NCCB's official position is that it cannot mandate the manner in which collection funds are handled within individual dioceses." That is canon law which is promulgated by the Holy See and applicable to all dioceses in the entire world. Even though you "cannot accept that excuse", the NCCB has no choice but to accept that as the universal law of the Church. Similarly, *Ex Corde Ecclesiae* is from the Canon law of the Church. It was that law that required the bishops of the United States to address that subject as they have.

Secondly, I think your letter and the enclosed pamphlet "Protecting the Parish Purse: a Roman Catholic Legacy of Neglect and Disgrace" from P.S. Services are intended to call our attention to a consulting service or product which would address the problem. Neither the letter nor the pamphlet specifically addressed that, but seems to be the point made in "The Rest of the Story."

If you or P.S. Services have either a product or a service which would be helpful to parishes, you may market those products or services directly to parishes or through dioceses.

Another way you may wish to approach this is by contacting the Diocesan Fiscal Management Conference, P.O. Box 199 Waterville, OH 43566-0199, and taking a booth at the annual meeting of the diocesan fiscal managers. This would provide you an opportunity to acquaint them with your services during the course of their annual meeting. While what you suggest cannot be done nationally, it could be done at the diocesan level, either voluntarily or by mandate in each diocese.

My years of experience with the Church have taught me that whenever a product or service does what it claims and is a value to the Church, it spreads like wild fire. It is for that reason that you see the same investment companies, auditors, church goods suppliers, etc., doing very well nationally. Good news travels fast.

Finally, as a piece of advice, if you are approaching this as a marketer, I would urge you to change the tone and approach of your material. I assure you that anyone in a parish or diocese who receives the pamphlet you sent to Bishop Fiorenza will become defensive. They will never get to the point of the letter discussing the product or service you have. I say this because I do not disagree with your analysis of the problem. However, most of those to whom you are directing this message will never read beyond the headline "A Roman Catholic Legacy of Neglect and Disgrace." Some might take it as offensive given the amount of work and effort they have already done in trying to improve internal control systems and accounting practices. No system of internal control is perfect. Even the U.S. Postal Service is plagued by breaches and embezzlements.

Very truly yours,

[name withheld], CPA

Associate General Secretary

[letterhead]

December 12, 1999

<u>PERSONAL ATTENTION</u>
[name withheld], CPA
Office of the General Secretary
National Conference of Catholic Bishops
3211 Fourth Street NE
Washington, DC 20017-1194

Dear [name withheld]:

Thank you for your letter of December 7 in response to my letter of November 28 to Bishop Fiorenza. Before addressing the contents of your letter, I would like to dispel an impression you apparently gained from my prior letter. Neither I nor P.S. Services is interested in marketing "a product or a service" although there was a time when that was true. The guidelines alluded to in my letter and enclosures were furnished the Conference in 1990 and have been available, <u>free</u>, via a download from my Website since March of this year. I am seeking fiscal and moral accountability, not monetary gain. Had you taken the time to visit my Website, you might have recognized that.

Since you raised the Canon Law defense, I took the time to research your statement that Canon Law precludes the Conference's involvement in the setting of standards for securing the Church's primary source of revenue: the Sunday collection. At the same time, I felt it appropriate to also research the legitimacy of my involvement. In that regard, Book II, Part I, Title I concerns <u>The Obligations and Rights of All Christ's Faithful</u> and Canon 212 §3 states as follows:

"They [Christ's Faithful] have the right, indeed at times the duty, in keeping with their knowledge, competence and position, to manifest to the sacred Pastors their views on matters which concern the good of the Church. They have the right also to make their views known to others of Christ's faithful, but in doing so they must always respect the integrity of faith and morals, show due reverence to the Pastors and take into account both the common good and the dignity of individuals." I hope you would

agree, that particular section affords me the right, perhaps even the obligation, to address the hierarchy regarding a condition I <u>know</u> has had and continues to have both an economically and morally debilitating effect upon the Church.

Concerning the Conference's authority to act in this matter, Book II, Part II, Section II, Title II, Chapter IV covers <u>Episcopal Conferences</u> and Canon 455 §1 states as follows:

"The Episcopal Conference can make general decrees only in cases where the universal law has so prescribed, or by special mandate of the Apostolic See, either on its own initiative or at the request of the Conference itself." As luck would have it, the "universal law" appears to so prescribe. Book V, Title I concerns <u>The Acquisition of Goods</u> and Canon 1265 §2 states: *"The Episcopal Conference can draw up rules regarding collections, which must be observed by all, including those who from their foundation are called and are 'mendicants'."* I trust the above citations dispel all questions regarding the Conference's authority as well as my right (duty) to cause them to act in this matter. Even absent Canon 1265 §2, the Conference would still have the option of requesting such authority from the Apostolic See per Canon 455 §1.

I do not believe any of your misstatements regarding Canon Law's application to this matter were intentional, but the fact that you were misinformed about what Canon Law does and does not permit should tell you something about the people for whom you work and the lengths to which they will go to avoid addressing the very critical, <u>Church-wide</u> issue of Sunday collection security. You mentioned my former agency, the U. S. Postal Service, as being "plagued by breaches and embezzlements." As information, the USPS has elaborate systems and procedures in place to both deter <u>and</u> detect employee embezzlements. The proof of that can be seen in the Postal Inspection Service's criminal statistics for FY 1998 which include 285 arrests as a result of financial investigations, many if not most of which were initiated on the basis of built-in indicators. As you probably know, the Church has no such substantive systems and procedures in place to deter or detect embezzlements.

In the last paragraph of your letter, you stated a great deal of work and effort has been directed toward improving "internal control systems and accounting practices." I don't dispute that claim, but how do you explain the fact that, despite all of that work and effort, the Church's primary source of revenue remains as vulnerable today as it was 25 or even 50 years ago? Given the abundance of financial experts (yourself included) at the Conference and diocesan levels, there's really only one logical explanation. Despite the relative ease and economy with which a secure system could be established, the very thought of a truly secure Sunday collection system is, for reasons best known to the hierarchy, anathema.

Amazingly, there is some good news in all of this. When I wrote Bishop Fiorenza, I knew only that my cause was logically, fiscally and morally sound. Thanks to your response, however, I now know that I and my cause are in concert with Canon Law. That was not your intention, of course, but after ten years of being made to feel like somewhat of an *intruder* - certainly a man without portfolio - you can't imagine how reassuring it is to know that I, one of Christ's Faithful, am properly engaged in a mission sanctioned by Canon Law and, by inference, the Apostolic See.

Sincerely,

Michael W. Ryan

cc: Most Reverend Joseph A. Fiorenza

[letterhead]

December 29, 1999

<u>PERSONAL AND CONFIDENTIAL</u>
Most Reverend Joseph A. Fiorenza
Bishop of Galveston-Houston
1700 San Jacinto
Houston, TX 77002-8291

Dear Bishop Fiorenza:

I have reason to believe you were never afforded an opportunity to review the enclosed November 28 letter. At the risk of sounding pompous, I believe it is the single most significant temporal call to action you will ever receive. Consequently, I am taking this means of ensuring that you at least see it; whether or not and how you choose to act upon it is a question that can only be resolved between you and your conscience.

If you delve into the history of this matter, Bishop Fiorenza, you will find that I have been the recipient of more dissembling from the NCCB than has the American public from the current administration. I have approached the topic of Sunday collection security from every angle imaginable only to be ignored or told absolute untruths. And until recently, I had no recourse or access to the media, the court of public opinion. Now, however, there is the World Wide Web, the Internet, where those who have been denied a fair hearing or, having been afforded a *hearing,* were ignored or dismissed in spite of having presented a solid case may make their case known to the general public. I have reluctantly elected to take advantage of that option.

In addition to my primary Website which offers a <u>free</u> download of <u>effective</u> collection security guidelines, I maintain several other sites including one devoted to the display of key correspondence and summaries which graphically illustrate the NCCB's 10-year role as the untouchable target in a game of *Dodge Ball.* The ball, of course, is <u>genuine</u> security which the Conference apparently loathes more that Lucifer himself. While that Website is relatively new, I expect visits to it will gradually increase among concerned Catholics and others as the various

Internet search engines assimilate its key words/phrases into their memory banks. If, for example, you were to conduct a search using the phrase "church collection security" (in quotes), it is quite likely that my several-year-old main Website will appear as the one and only result. I hope to achieve a similar level of recognition with the NCCB-related Website.

I look forward to hearing from you, Bishop Fiorenza, and I stand ready to assist in any way possible.

Most sincerely,

Michael W. Ryan

enclosures (4)

[letterhead]

March 10, 2000

<u>PERSONAL AND CONFIDENTIAL</u>
Most Reverend Joseph A. Fiorenza
Bishop of Galveston-Houston
1700 San Jacinto
Houston, TX 77002-8291

Dear Bishop Fiorenza:

This refers to my letters of November 28 and December 29, 1999 concerning the Church's failure to afford an adequate level of protection for its principal source of revenue: the Sunday collection. Copies of those letters as well as copies of correspondence previously submitted with them are herewith.

I am now in the process of preparing a petition which will be transmitted to the Holy See, and I am wondering if you wish to remain characterized therein as the third NCCB President who chose to stand mute and allow the thoroughly discredited response of a subordinate to represent his position on the topics of revenue protection, embezzlement and unnecessary temptation within the U. S. Catholic Church. If so, your decision puts you in the company of two prior Presidents: Cardinal Keeler and Bishop Pilarczyk. Only your immediate predecessor, Bishop Anthony Pilla, deemed the subject to be of sufficient importance to warrant his personal attention.

Being, as we are, in the Lenten season of the year in which our Holy Father has issued a call for Church-wide apology and atonement, it would appear to be both timely and appropriate for the hierarchy you represent to acknowledge that a vulnerable Sunday collection system constitutes a great temptation to sin which can and should be neutralized through the implementation of readily available, low-cost security systems and procedures. Continuation of the NCCB's evasive and disingenuous treatment of this critical issue is inexcusable and renders suspect the sincerity of their pronouncements on other subjects. You need only review the case of Rev. [name withheld] to know this issue has compelling moral implications.

I look forward to hearing from you, Bishop Fiorenza. As I have advised every prelate with whom I've corresponded in my ten-year quest for corrective action, I stand ready to assist the NCCB in achieving this moral and fiscal objective in any way the Conference may deem appropriate.

Most sincerely,

Michael W. Ryan

enclosures (4)

[letterhead]

April 4, 2000

<u>PERSONAL ATTENTION</u>
[name withheld]
Office of the General Secretary
National Conference of Catholic Bishops
3211 Fourth Street NE
Washington, DC 20017-1194

Dear [name withheld]:

I received your letter of March 27 in response to my March 10 letter to Bishop Fiorenza. While the fact that any bishops would gather for the specific purpose of discussing accountability is encouraging, I remain only cautiously optimistic regarding the likelihood of a positive outcome. Nevertheless, I offer the following additional references and information and respectfully request that it be included in the participants' informational packets.

In addition to the canons cited in my letter of December 12, I respectfully suggest the bishops include the following canon in their deliberations: Book V, Title II, Canon 1284, §1 and §2, 1° and 4° which read in pertinent part as follows: *All administrators are to perform their duties with the diligence of a good householder. Therefore they must: 1° be vigilant that no goods placed in their care <u>in any way</u> perish or suffer damage . . . 4° . . . <u>guard them securely</u>* . . . (emphasis added)

Canon law also emphasizes the need to comply with applicable civil laws. In that regard, my Webster's unabridged Second Edition defines *nonfeasance* as follows: *"in law, a failure to perform a duty"*. In light of the Canon 1284, I respectfully suggest the bishops' ongoing and willful refusal to implement detailed, genuinely secure procedures oriented toward the protection of <u>undeposited</u> Sunday collection funds appears to meet that definition. In support of that, I refer to the following standards promulgated by your own professional society, the American Institute of Certified Public Accountants.

In 1972 the AICPA issued an authoritative guideline entitled *Statement on Auditing Standards - Codification of Auditing Standards and Procedures.* Of particular note for churches is Section 320.44 which states, in pertinent part: ". . . *agreement of a cash count with the recorded balance does not provide evidence that all cash received has been properly recorded. This illustrates an unavoidable distinction between <u>fiduciary</u> and recorded <u>accountability</u>: the former arises immediately upon acquisition of an asset; the latter arises only when the initial record of the transaction is prepared.*" (emphasis added)

In the case of a church's Sunday collection, fiduciary accountability begins when members of the congregation place their offerings in the collection basket. In a typical parish, however, the number of people (clergy, employees and volunteers) having lone, unobserved access to the collection or a portion thereof prior to its tabulation and deposit (*recorded accountability*) would leave even the greenest of auditors aghast. Section 320.42 of the AICPA statement addresses that critical interval, declaring: "*The objective of safeguarding assets requires that access be limited to authorized personnel. The number and caliber of personnel to whom access is authorized should be influenced by <u>the nature of the assets and the related susceptibility to loss through errors and irregularities</u>. Limitation of direct access to assets <u>requires</u> appropriate physical segregation and protective equipment or devices.*" (emphasis added)

The terms <u>errors</u> and <u>irregularities</u> are employed to differentiate between accidental and intentional wrongdoing, respectively. When one considers "*the nature of the assets*" involved, i.e., significant amounts of <u>uncounted</u> currency, their "*related susceptibility to loss*" as a result of intentional wrongdoing should be glaringly evident to any knowledgeable and objective reviewer.

Many churches have good or perhaps even excellent control over their cash disbursements and thus might conclude that their revenue is secure. Section 320.67 of the AICPA statement addresses that misconception, in pertinent part, as follows: "*Controls and weaknesses affecting different classes of transactions are not offsetting in their effect. For example, <u>weaknesses in cash receipts procedures are not mitigated by controls in cash disbursements procedures</u> . . .*" (emphasis added) For a church, of course, the "*cash receipts procedures*" are represented by all stages of the Sunday collection process up to and including the bank deposit.

It is also relevant to note that, for those organizations whose continued existence depends upon their ability to show a financial profit, new technology and more efficient procedures are quickly adopted whenever such action is seen as a way to improve the so-called *bottom line.* But churches and other nonprofit organizations lack the *for profit* motive, and that absence can serve to strengthen, even institutionalize, that old rationale which usually concludes with the expression "*because this is the way we've always done it.*" Any church officials who recognize they might fit into that category would be well advised to heed the AICPA's overview of management's fiscal responsibilities as stated in Section 110.02: "*Management has the responsibility for adopting sound accounting policies, for maintaining an adequate and effective system of accounts, for safeguarding assets, and for devising a system of internal control that will, among other things, help assure the production of proper financial statements.*"

Finally, and at the risk of antagonizing the participants, I respectfully direct your attention to two of Jesus' admonitions. I believe both of them bear directly upon this matter.

> Matthew 18:7 - "*Things that make people fall into sin are bound to happen, but how terrible for the one who makes them happen.*"

> Luke 12:2-3 - "*Whatever is covered up will be uncovered, and every secret will be made known. So then, whatever you have said in the dark will be heard in broad daylight, and whatever you have whispered in private in a closed room will be shouted from the housetops.*"

While the bishops did not cause this temptation to sin, its elimination is totally within their power. In my opinion, their steadfast refusal to do so renders them subject to the spirit of Matthew 18:7. Insofar as Luke and Sunday collection security are concerned, I have no doubt that, over the past decade, many thoughts have been expressed *in the dark* and many opinions have been *whispered in private*, thoughts and opinions which the participants would never wish to be *shouted from the housetops*. I pray your meeting will be conducted as though our Lord were present in body as well as in spirit. In that circumstance, I am hopeful the extraneous considerations which affected past deliberations will dissipate in the face of logic, common sense and an overwhelming desire to do what is best for Christ's faithful.

After ten years, [name withheld], it should go without saying but I once again wish to declare my readiness to assist the bishops in any way they may deem appropriate. In that regard, my Website (http://www.gis.net/~pss) contains a great deal of information, including a synopsis of the elements of a genuinely secure collection system as well as detailed guidelines for establishing that condition. I would appreciate being informed of the outcome of your meeting at such time as the results become available.

Sincerely,

Michael W. Ryan

cc: Bishop Fiorenza

[letterhead]

June 15, 2000

<u>PERSONAL ATTENTION</u>
[name withheld]
Office of the General Secretary
National Conference of Catholic Bishops
3211 Fourth Street NE
Washington, DC 20017-1194

Dear [name withheld]:

This refers to your letter of March 27 in which you advised that you were *"meeting with a group of bishops in April to discuss accountability and the canons which are applicable"* to my contention that the U.S. hierarchy is not affording an adequate level of protection for its principal source of revenue: the Sunday collection. I acknowledged your letter via Certified Mail on April 4, referencing what I felt were relevant canons and requesting that I be informed of the outcome. As you know, my immediate interest in the outcome is due to the fact that I am in the process of preparing a detailed petition which will be directed to the Holy See, and I want to be sure that it conveys the Conference's current position and rationale as accurately as possible.

In the absence of any notification from you concerning that meeting, I am once again asking to be informed of the outcome. In all fairness to you, however, I feel obliged to inform you that Bishop Fiorenza's reticence and our correspondence to date (yours and mine) will form the introduction to my petition. Further, you surely recognize that Bishop Fiorenza has remained silent not only out of disdain for me and what he views as my lack of portfolio but also because it is impossible to defend the indefensible. We all know there neither is nor can be any ethical or moral basis for leaving the Sunday collection vulnerable to repetitive (weekly) embezzlement when, with minimal expense and effort, it can be made genuinely secure.

I assume the referenced meeting did not result in a decision to move toward nationwide establishment of a genuinely secure Sunday collection system. In that case, you will be well advised to ensure that any reply you make is true to the best traditions of your profession.

Clearly, your employers' position on the matter of Sunday collection security is antithetical to the principles and standards of the American Institute of Certified Public Accountants, not to mention the commonly accepted understanding of *nonfeasance* in the business world and courts of law.

Copies of this letter are being directed to Bishop Fiorenza at both his Washington and Houston offices. I would greatly appreciate his personal opinion but trust that any reply you give will have the concurrence of General Secretary [name withheld] and/or General Secretary-Elect [name withheld].

Sincerely,

Michael W. Ryan

cc: Bishop Joseph A. Fiorenza, President, NCCB

[letterhead]

April 22, 2001

<u>PERSONAL ATTENTION</u>
His Excellency, Archbishop Csaba Ternyak
Secretary, Congregation for the Clergy
00120 Citta del Vaticano
Rome, Italy

RE: Prot. N. 20010612

Dear Archbishop Ternyak;

I received your letter of March 30 in reply to my letter of February 14 to His Eminence, Joseph Cardinal Ratzinger, Prefect of the *Sacred Congregation for the Doctrine of Faith.* As you know, that letter was accompanied by a 4-page petition and more than 100 pages of exhibits pertaining to "the interrelated matters of repetitive, surreptitious theft, and the sins and occasions of sin generated and countenanced by an intentionally vulnerable revenue handling process." Together, the petition and exhibits clearly establish the adverse moral ramifications of the status quo as well as the U. S. Episcopal Conference's deliberate refusal to initiate corrective action.

In light of the overriding moral consequences of preserving the status quo with respect to current Sunday collection procedures in the American Catholic Church, I was surprised to receive a reply from the *Congregation for the Clergy.* That surprise turned to near disbelief, however, when I read your four-sentence reply which acknowledged receipt of my letter alone and avoided any mention of the heart of my petition: the sins and occasions of sin which flow from an intentionally vulnerable revenue handling process. I trust your decision to ignore the overriding moral issue was not in any way influenced by the fact that fully two thirds of the case histories included with my petition relate to thefts by members of the clergy.

If my objective had been to prove that the hierarchy of our Church will adopt any position that will enable them to avoid taking action to correct the perennial evil of Sunday collection theft, you could not have been more helpful. Given the documentation included with my petition, your proffer of the rationale that "*security of the 'Sunday Collection' is something that would fall under the competency of the local Bishop*" is an insult to your intelligence as well as it is to mine. Indeed, it suggests that the examination which formed the basis for your letter was performed by a subordinate. If that is the case, I must say you were poorly served by that individual.

My petition does not concern the "competency" of local bishops. If you read my petition, Your Excellency, you know at least three things: 1.) the phenomenon of embezzlement from the Sunday collection is (at least in America) a Church-wide, multi-million dollar, perennial plague; 2.) it is a major source of serious sin; and 3.) Canon Law specifically provides that Episcopal Conferences may issue rules regarding collections, which rules "*must be observed by all*". It is therefore illogical (at best) to hold or imply that the problem is best handled by local bishops.

In light of the aforementioned, Archbishop Ternyak, I respectfully request that my petition and the many relevant exhibits which accompanied it be reexamined. While I remain convinced that the matter would be best addressed by the *Sacred Congregation for the Doctrine of Faith*, I assume the Prefect of your Congregation, His Eminence, Dario Cardinal Castrillon-Hoyos, is empowered to initiate action that could culminate with implementation of the centralized corrective measures that are so clearly and desperately needed. I pray that you and Cardinal Castrillon-Hoyos will not let the fact that such measures could and should have been implemented several decades ago deter you from initiating that long-overdue action at this time.

If, upon prayerful reflection, you and Cardinal Castrillon-Hoyos decide not to reexamine my petition, I would greatly appreciate it if you would at least refer a copy of the petition and transmittal letter to the appropriate official of the U. S. Conference of Catholic Bishops. I ask this because those documents contain one or more relevant points that were not presented to the U. S. Conference in any of my prior communications. Although (based upon more than ten years of fruitless communication) I have little hope that anything positive will come from that referral, there is always a possibility that the Holy Spirit will descend upon the recipient and instill in him a right judgment, a clear insight and a courageous resolve to boldly address this critical area which remains so vitally important to the moral and fiscal well-being of our Church.

Most sincerely,

Michael W. Ryan

cc: His Eminence Joseph Cardinal Ratzinger
    Sacred Congregation for the Doctrine of Faith

[letterhead]

November 23, 2001

PERSONAL AND CONFIDENTIAL
Most Reverend Wilton D. Gregory
Bishop, Diocese of Belleville
222 South Third Street
Belleville, IL 62220

Dear Bishop Gregory:

Congratulations on your recent election to serve as President of the U. S. Conference of Catholic Bishops. I wish you every success during your tenure which, as you know only too well, comes at a time when religious beliefs have moved to *center stage* in our very troubled world.

The purpose of my letter, Bishop Gregory, is to call to your attention a long-standing condition that has serious implications for our religious beliefs, the Church's fiscal viability in the 21st century, and the U. S. Conference's ability to claim the moral high ground on public issues. It's not my intention to blind-side you, however, so I must advise you on the front end that I have corresponded with at least four of your predecessors on this subject: the protection of Sunday collection funds. What makes my contact with you somewhat unique, however, is the fact that it is my first contact since experiencing a most disheartening exchange with the Holy See.

Enclosed are copies of a transmittal letter and four-page petition that were directed to His Eminence Joseph Cardinal Ratzinger, Prefect of the Sacred Congregation of the Faith on February 14, 2001. It contains the details of my position, most of which have been called to the attention of your predecessors over the course of the past eleven years. Unfortunately, Cardinal Ratzinger (or his staff) referred my petition to the Congregation for the Clergy who declined to question the U. S. Conference's thoroughly disproved stance, merely parroting the USCCB position that such matters cannot be handled at the Conference level and are therefore left to local bishops.

At such time as you have had an opportunity to review these documents, Bishop Gregory, I would greatly appreciate hearing from you. I know how busy you must be, but I believe this matter, because of its strong moral and fiscal ramifications, warrants your personal attention. At this time, the issue is only known to a handful of my associates and members of the Conference. However, I intend to publicize this glaring example of nonfeasance as widely as possible until such time as the USCCB recants and moves to eliminate this blight on the U. S. Church and its faithful. In that regard, I invite you to visit my newly established website, *www.ChurchSecurity.info.*

Most sincerely,

Michael W. Ryan

Office of the President

3211 FOURTH STREET NE. WASHINGTON DC 20017-1194
202-541-3100 Fax 202-541-3166
Most Reverend Wilton D. Gregory, S.L.D.
Bishop of Belleville

December 10, 2001

Dear Mr. Ryan:

Your letter of November 23, 2001 led me to ask for a briefing from our Conference staff about the matter you raised and the history of its discussion with my predecessors. As President of the Bishops' Conference, I am interested in a broad range of issues which affect the Church in this country, and as a diocesan Bishop I share the concern you have about the integrity and safety of our Sunday collections. But I am also mindful of the autonomy of the diocesan Bishop and what can and cannot be legislated or required from the national level.

I concur with the expressions of my predecessors and the Conference staff that we are not empowered either canonically or by our Conference statutes and bylaws to address the question of internal controls over offertory collections in such a way as to standardize or require any particular procedures.

However, as a Bishops' Conference, we can, and have, encouraged dioceses to practice good accounting practices and internal controls. As diocesan Bishops, we rely heavily on our finance officers and finance councils to assist us in exercising our own stewardship and providing guidance to our pastors.

I think the points you make are best directed to the fiscal officers, and for that reason I am going to send a copy of your letter to the Diocesan Fiscal Management Conference. They meet annually and address these issues with the encouragement of their bishops and from their unique vantage point in their dioceses. I trust that they will look at your website, www.ChurchSecurity.info, and study your letter with the good of the Church in mind. They can consider the lived experiences of the local churches and how they might best assist all the fiscal managers in evaluating their local controls.

With gratitude for your scholarship and presentation and with every best wish for a blessed Advent, I am

Sincerely yours in Christ,

Most Reverend Wilton D. Gregory

Bishop of Belleville

President

cc: Reverend [name withheld], DFMC

[letterhead]

January 14, 2002

<u>PERSONAL AND CONFIDENTIAL</u>
Most Reverend Wilton D. Gregory, S.L.D.
USCCB President and Bishop of Belleville
222 South Third Street
Belleville, IL 62220

Dear Bishop Gregory:

I received your letter of December 10 and wish to begin by thanking you for your prompt and thoughtful reply concerning the matter of Sunday collection security in the American Church. I was surprised, however, to hear you repeat a position I am satisfied is incorrect, i.e., that the U.S. Conference is not canonically empowered "to address the question of internal controls over offertory collections". In research conducted last year, I found Canon Law specifically empowers any conference to do so. <u>Book V, Title I, Canon 1265 §2</u> states: *"The Episcopal Conference can draw up rules regarding collections, which must be observed by all"*. As the general meaning of that section seems quite clear, I am left to wonder if there exists a special Canon Law exception that prohibits the U. S. Conference from availing itself of that all-encompassing authority?

Assuming no such exception has been made (it would certainly represent a slap in the face of the U. S. Conference if it had), I am left with your reference to *Conference statutes and bylaws* and that, as you might suspect, is the crux of the matter. Whatever the specifics of those statutes and bylaws might be, their ultimate effect (well-known to all key members of the Conference) is to institutionalize a perennial evil as old as the Church itself. I am, of course, referring to Sunday collection theft which I believe, aside from the priest-pedophile phenomenon, is the single greatest Catholic Church scandal of the 20th Century. Sadly, my eleven-year effort to promote low-cost, readily available corrective measures notwithstanding, the American Church is now well into the 21st Century with that evil still firmly in place and, from all appearances, fully USCCB approved.

I could go into further detail, Bishop Gregory, but you already have a copy of my Vatican petition and access to my website, *www.ChurchSecurity.info* which provides everything you ever wanted to know and then some. That brings me to the DFMC and [name withheld] who, with the possible exception of Sr. Frances Mlocek, might well be the most ethical member of your staff. To put it in context for you, Sr. Mlocek referred me to [name withheld], then Executive Director of the DFMC, in early 1994. Concurrently, she also referred our (by then) extensive correspondence file to [name withheld]. On January 11, 1994, I directed a two-page letter to [name withheld]. Not only did he fail to provide a substantive response, he did not even acknowledge receipt or my letter.

At the time, I chalked it up to arrogance and poor upbringing but, upon reflection, I have since concluded he did the only thing he could to both retain his position with the Conference and preserve his integrity. Given his background and experience, [name withheld] had to have seen and understood the position I have consistently held: that the Sunday collection in the average parish is as vulnerable as a newborn babe, and that it remains so as a direct result of the Conference's knowing and willful refusal to avail itself of low-cost security measures that have been available for decades if not generations. His dilemma: acknowledge the truth and *fail* the hierarchy; deny the truth and fail himself. His solution: completely ignore the intruder.

So I'm left with this question, Bishop Gregory: why would the Conference engage in more than a decade of dissembling and obfuscation to ensure that hundreds (probably thousands) of Sunday collection thieves can continue their unfettered, sinful thievery week after week and year after year? While you and your brother bishops are in the best position to answer that question, the following is my theory, based upon both my personal and professional experience.

Considering only the embezzlement case histories I have accumulated over the past ten years, it appears fully two thirds of the publicly identified embezzlers are members of the clergy. Further, I know many pastors supplement their income with a weekly pre-deposit deduction from the Sunday collection. Some consider it *Petty Cash* when, in fact, it doesn't even come close to meeting that criteria. In any event, a truly secure Sunday collection system would not permit any such deductions, and that policy would almost certainly be poorly received at the parish level. Indeed, many pastors would either refuse to implement secure procedures or would modify them (thus rendering them flawed) to ensure the continuation of their supplemental income. And then, of course, there is the matter of sudden increases in Sunday collection funds when such increases are directly attributable to the implementation of secure procedures. How do we handle that with the media without admitting the Church had a serious theft problem?

Well, that almost sounds like a very good reason to forgo secure procedures, doesn't it? We know it isn't, of course. Refusal to implement secure procedures under that scenario can be likened to cowardice in the face of the enemy who, in this case, just happens to be Satan himself. What amazes me, Bishop Gregory, is the fact that our shepherds (the USCCB membership) have been and remain to this day so willing to turn their backs on their flock, allowing the wolves to have their way, just so they (our shepherds) can avoid making the morally correct but (from the clergy's perspective) unpopular decision that would all but eliminate the repetitive sin of Sunday collection theft while, at the same time, restoring <u>millions</u> of dollars in lost revenue <u>annually</u>.

If I have failed to convince you of the absolute need for concerted and authoritative action in this matter, Bishop Gregory, I hope you will someday find the words to explain your rationale. As matters stand, I am left with the strong belief that our hierarchy is substantially (perhaps even overwhelmingly) comprised of self-centered, secular rulers. As harsh as that opinion may seem, I read of the Holy Father's request (in connection with a recent conclave) wherein he called upon all bishops to examine their lifestyles and ensure they are in full concert with the model of humility and selfless service recommended and exemplified by our Lord. That request lead me to conclude His Holiness has seen evidence of worldly lifestyles among those who have been entrusted with the task of preserving and spreading the Good News, and I respectfully suggest that conclusion is supported by the U.S. Conference's ongoing refusal to implement genuinely secure procedures.

Most sincerely,

Michael W. Ryan

[letterhead]

April 24, 2002

<u>PERSONAL AND CONFIDENTIAL</u>
Most Reverend Wilton D. Gregory, S.L.D.
USCCB President and Bishop of Belleville
222 South Third Street
Belleville, IL 62220

Dear Bishop Gregory:

This refers to my letters of November 23, 2001 and January 14, 2002 concerning the U.S. Conference's ongoing refusal to provide an adequate level of protection for the Church's primary source of revenue, the Sunday collection. While you have yet to respond to my January 14 letter, I assume it is because your attention has been focused on the only matter that eclipses the Sunday collection issue in terms of its overall importance: the predator-priest scandal. However, as it is possible that letter went astray, I am attaching a copy as information.

While this may seem like *piling on,* I believe it is both appropriate and timely to elucidate some parallels between the predator-priest scandal and the Conference's refusal (falsely attributed to overriding local autonomy) to implement uniform procedures which will ensure that each and every dollar that is placed in the collection basket is, <u>in fact</u>, deposited in the parish bank account.

First, there is the decades-old tendency of the hierarchy to place image ahead of substance. Cases of reported sexual abuse were addressed with confidential financial settlements, ineffective treatments and convenient transfers by responsible bishops, archbishops and cardinals whose main objective was to avoid negative publicity. The same can be said for Sunday collection thefts, especially when the thief is a member of the clergy. One of the best and most recent examples is that of Rev. [name withheld] who is credited with stealing well over $1 million dollars over the course of his 26-year career. And what did he do with that money? He financed a lavish lifestyle for himself and his secretary with whom he had lived for a number of years. Think about the cause and effect aspect of that scandal; if he (and his secretary) had not had such easy access to Sunday collection funds, would he have gone off the proverbial *deep end* as he clearly did?

[His] case is not an anomaly. Other examples include the cases of [name withheld], [name withheld], [name withheld], [name withheld], [name withheld], [name withheld], [name withheld], [name withheld], [name withheld] and [name withheld], all of whom once held the title "Reverend". All of these cases (and many more secreted in diocesan files) were labeled isolated occurrences because no one in the hierarchy wanted to admit there is an inherent weakness in the way the Church handles its principal source of revenue. Why is the hierarchy so loath to openly recognize that fact? Because once they admit it, they become obligated to implement corrective measures, and that's the last thing they want to do. They know many priests are supplementing their admittedly meager incomes from undocumented collection funds and, rather than address that issue, the Conference members merely turn a blind eye to the illegal and immoral alternative.

And that brings me to the next item: the sin of theft (not to mention the sins that follow it) and who is ultimately responsible for that sin when it is facilitated by the Conference's conscious, knowing and willful decision to abide the tempting conditions which lead to it. If it is true that one can be guilty of a sin of omission, might it be said that deliberate refusal to eradicate a specific temptation to sin, when it is well within one's power to do so, would constitute a sin of omission? And if that is true, does it not follow that the Conference's refusal to secure the Sunday collection is a sin of omission and thus makes them ultimately responsible for the thefts committed <u>weekly</u> by those who are unable to resist the temptation presented by highly vulnerable collection funds? I firmly believe it does.

On many occasions in past correspondence with a number of your predecessors and other members of the USCCB, Bishop Gregory, I've cited certain audit and financial security standards promulgated by the American Institute of Certified Public Accountants, and not once has anyone challenged either their accuracy or their applicability to the Sunday collection. This is especially telling since I have always stated that they clearly and unequivocally establish that the hierarchy is not fulfilling its responsibility to protect the Church's primary source of revenue. All I have ever gotten in reply is the spurious claim that the Conference is not empowered to act, or that the respondent believes *present procedures are adequate.* The latter statement has been made even though it was clear no substantive procedures even existed.

If the Church as represented by the USCCB is truly committed to reform the way in which it addresses internal misconduct, with a view toward putting the good of the flock ahead of image and expediency, it will initiate a high-level study group to consider the issue of Sunday collection theft and its impact on the fiscal and moral health of the U. S. Catholic Church. If that isn't done, I and anyone I share my extensive files with will know the only reason the Conference is presently addressing the predator-priest scandal is the extensive publicity that has been given it and that it is not due to any sense of honor or moral outrage. The Sunday collection scandal may not blossom in the media during your tenure, Bishop Gregory, but it will blossom one day and you, along with several of your peers and predecessors, will be remembered as the ones who turned a blind eye.

Finally, Bishop Gregory, I want to assure you that I am not one of those who are bound and determined to turn the Church upside down. My wife and I are active members of St. [name withheld]. We have lived in seven states and have been actively involved in most of the parishes we have lived in. Our involvement includes Eucharistic Minister, Pre Cana, Religious Education, Lector and, of course, Sunday collection counting. Feel free to contact our present pastor, Rev. [name withheld], to confirm our involvement and support for our parish and diocese.

I look forward to hearing from you and wish to assure you of my continuing desire to assist the Conference in any way it feels I can be most useful.

Most sincerely,

Michael W. Ryan

[letterhead]

January 20, 2004

<u>PERSONAL AND CONFIDENTIAL</u>
Most Reverend Wilton D. Gregory, S.L.D.
President, U. S. Conference of Catholic Bishops
3211 Fourth Street NE
Washington, DC 20017-1194

Dear Bishop Gregory:

This refers to my letters of November 23, 2001 and January 14 and April 22, 2002 concerning the need to establish and implement uniform procedures to protect the Church's primary source of revenue, the Sunday collection. While you did not respond to my last two letters, I nevertheless feel obliged to make one final attempt to explain - in the clearest possible terms - what I view to be the implications and ramifications of the USCCB's ongoing failure to act in this matter.

To begin with, however, I must return to your letter of December 10, 2001 in which you stated: "*we are not empowered either canonically or by our Conference statutes and bylaws to address the question of internal controls over offertory collections in such a way as to standardize or require any particular procedures.*" Accepting the strict accuracy of that statement, I would then ask you whether there is a procedure by which the Conference could become so empowered. As you must know, Canon 455 provides that a conference may seek authorization to issue a *general decree* which, if granted, may be imposed following approval by 2/3 of the Conference members. In light of that, I trust you will concede that what we are really talking about here is not what the USCCB can or cannot require of its members but rather what it does or does not wish to require and, in this case, it does not wish to require genuinely secure Sunday collection procedures.

I imagine your second line of defense is that "*the autonomy of the diocesan Bishop*" is paramount. Assuming that fairly captures the essence of your thinking, we should now examine the condition that has been perpetuated, even institutionalized, to preserve the bishops' *autonomy.*

Absent national standards, the best that can be said is that the level of security over collection funds varies from diocese to diocese and from parish to parish within each diocese. I contend it's worse than that. I believe none of the almost 200 dioceses have implemented procedures which effectively preclude covert theft between collection basket and parish bank deposit and all points in-between. If you know of one that has, please identify it so that I might request (with your endorsement) a copy of their procedures. If you will stipulate that a vulnerable Sunday collection constitutes a temptation to sin (to steal), and that a perpetually vulnerable Sunday collection is an ongoing temptation to sin, it follows that, in opting not to seek authority to issue a *general decree* implementing procedures that would virtually eliminate that temptation to sin, the bishops are placing *executive privilege* ahead of what can quite reasonably be described as a moral obligation to eliminate a great temptation to sin and a source of actual, ongoing sin within the Church itself.

In a January 16 press conference held to express the Church's opposition to gay marriage, Bishop Coleman of Fall River affirmed that "*we will have to answer to God for anything we fail to do.*" It is ironic that those who were responsible for crafting the language of the new catechism, particularly #2287, are themselves among the most flagrant of its violators. I can't imagine any circumstance that could justify the Conference's inaction (nonfeasance) in this matter. If you know of one, I would greatly appreciate your letting me know the nature of that circumstance.

After reportedly likening some secretive bishops to the Mafia in a Los Angeles Times interview, I understand Governor Keating stated in his letter of resignation to you that "*To resist grand jury subpoenas, to suppress the names of offending clerics, to deny, to obfuscate, to explain away; that is a model of a criminal organization, not my church.*" Not being as erudite as Governor Keating, it took me several years of fruitless interaction to reach essentially the same conclusion. If the USCCB has learned nothing else from the predator-priest scandal, surely it has learned that obfuscation and dissembling are antithetical to the role of a shepherd of Christ.

I would therefore like to believe that, had your letter been written on December 10, 2003, your response would have been vastly different. I would like to believe you would have said (in so many words) *"You're absolutely right, Mr. Ryan, the Sunday collection is as vulnerable as a newborn babe and thereby a great temptation to sin for which we bishops must accept full responsibility. In my capacity as President of the USCCB, I am going to place this subject at the top of the agenda for our next convocation and I will do everything in my power to see that this blight on our integrity is eliminated as quickly as possible. Toward that end, I am directing Rev. [name withheld] to immediately create a blue-ribbon ad hoc committee to study your collection security guidelines and to develop a system that will equal or exceed the standards contained therein."*

This issue is not going to disappear in our lifetime, Bishop Gregory, and with all due respect, I do not believe all the good you have done in your life, as lofty and considerable as it surely must be, will compensate for your having knowingly and willfully opted not to take the action you have to know in your innermost being should be taken without further delay. Toward that end, I pray the Holy Spirit will descend upon you and instill within you the wisdom and courage that will surely be needed to see this truly Church-defining crisis through to its proper conclusion.

In conclusion, I invite your attention to the enclosed news article and pose the following question. Could you, as a member and President of the USCCB, have initiated action that could have kept that pathetic individual from plundering his parish's Sunday collection? Clearly, his ready access to Sunday collection funds facilitated his other sinful behaviors. As much as I will have to answer for on Judgment Day, I can honestly say I did everything within my power to prevent that tragedy and others like it. Can you and your brother bishops make the same statement?

Most Sincerely,

Michael W. Ryan

enclosure

[letterhead]

January 3, 2006

<u>PERSONAL ATTENTION</u>
Most Reverend William S. Skylstad, President
U.S. Conference of Catholic Bishops
3211 Fourth Street, N.E.
Washington, D.C. 20017-1104

Dear Bishop Skylstad:

I am writing this letter with little hope it will elicit the response I believe our Lord would expect of one of His disciples. Indeed, based upon my past experience, I realize those charged with responsibility for screening your correspondence might well refer this letter to an underling who will take it upon himself to either *deep-six* the letter or reply with the kind of disingenuous verbiage I have received in the past. Nevertheless, I feel a moral obligation to my fellow Catholics to make the effort.

The subject of my concern is church revenue protection which, at the parish level, is virtually non-existent. In what has been an unsuccessful 16-year effort to correct that intolerable condition, I have presented the case for <u>effective</u> revenue protection measures to each of your predecessors dating back to Bishop Pilarczyk. This present effort is different, however; since I last corresponded with your immediate predecessor, Bishop Gregory, I have had two articles published in the Catholic periodical *New Oxford Review,* and I am presently working on a third article which will draw upon the themes of the first two and, in effect, clearly and firmly establish responsibility for the lack of secure procedures squarely in the lap of the USCCB. The first two articles (*The Second Greatest Scandal in the Church* and *Post-Deposit Embezzlements*) are available for download at my website: ChurchSecurity.info.

In light of the above, Bishop Skylstad, I strongly and respectfully encourage you to have a member of your staff download the referenced articles for your review. Between the two, you will have a clear picture of the case I have been fruitlessly attempting to make for the past 16 years. I firmly believe anyone who reads those articles with an open mind can only reach one conclusion: that an immediate, <u>Church-wide</u> overhaul of the way funds are handled at the parish level is a moral and fiscal imperative.

That brings me to the crux of past evasions and roadblocks: the Conference's authority to mandate uniform standards upon its member dioceses. Canon Law provides a mechanism for obtaining Vatican approval for Conference-wide mandates that then only require two-thirds approval of its members. If you take the position that the members will not approve Conference-wide security measures, you are (in effect) saying most bishops prefer to keep parish revenue <u>highly</u> vulnerable to theft. For more on that, see my January 20, 2004 letter to then USCCB President Bishop Wilton Gregory.

In any event, I look forward to hearing from you after you have had time to fully contemplate this critical issue.

Most sincerely,

Michael W. Ryan

enclosures (2)

[letterhead]

December 17, 2007

<u>PERSONAL ATTENTION</u>
Francis Cardinal George, President
U. S. Conference of Catholic Bishops
3211 Fourth Street, N.E.
Washington, D.C. 20017

Dear Cardinal George:

To begin, I extend my congratulations and best wishes on your election to succeed Bishop Skylstad as President of the USCCB. While I am not a historian, I believe the Catholic Church has never in my lifetime been in a more precarious position than that in which it rests today, and it is encouraging to me to know that your peers chose you, in particular, to represent the Church in America.

By way of introduction, I am the original author of the Sunday collection guidelines implemented by the AD of Chicago in early 2005 via the guideline entitled *Management of Sunday Collections*. As far as I know, the AD of Chicago is the first U. S. diocese to implement my guidelines, and I congratulate you and your Department of Finance for having the wisdom to recognize the need for such guidelines, and the courage to implement them.

I'm sure the guidelines were met with opposition from a number of clergy and lay persons who either felt insulted by their implications or had a vested interest in keeping the Sunday collection vulnerable. No doubt Rev. [name withheld] had a few choice words for you or your CFO when the guidelines were issued.

Regarding the case of Rev. [name withheld], however, it is important to note that even after the guidelines were implemented, he was able to carry on his embezzlement due to the lack of one key element of my guidelines that was not carried forward in yours: the requirement that collection bag serial numbers be recorded when they are put out for use by the ushers and later compared against the serial numbers recorded by the counters to ensure that the the two are in agreement. My guidelines express that simple yet vital step in a single sentence: *"The secretary or other designee will later compare the serial numbers of the opened seals against the serial numbers recorded separately by the person who assigned them for use by the ushers."* It is apparent from the [name withheld] case that our guidelines (mine and yours) need to place greater emphasis on that critical procedure and verification; in all likelihood, other wayward clergy and laity are availing themselves of that vulnerability as I type this letter.

Now, if I haven't already lost your interest, Eminence, I would like to share with you my concern for the USCCB's ongoing failure to implement genuinely secure Sunday collection procedures <u>nationwide</u>. This is an issue I have called to the attention of every President from Archbishop Pilarczyk to Bishop Skylstad, sadly, to no avail. If your first impulse at this point is to refer this letter to [name withheld] or some other member of the staff who has been preconditioned to reply with the *we-are-not-empowered*, (we being the USCCB) and the *prerogatives-of-each-bishop* excuses, I implore you to reconsider.

You have seen first-hand what it takes to protect Sunday collections from the depredations of a determined embezzler, and you know in your heart there is no legitimate reason in the world why the USCCB cannot agree on a universal set of guidelines. To take the position that the autonomy and prerogatives of individual bishops is paramount is to place executive privilege ahead of what can quite reasonably be described as a moral obligation to eliminate a great temptation to sin (Sunday collection theft) and a known source of ongoing sin within the Church itself. And while that prioritization is not foreign to the corporate world, it's not what one would expect to see in any Christian denomination, and most especially not in the Catholic Church that so proudly traces its lineage to Jesus himself.

Based upon your personal knowledge of the secure procedures in effect within your own Archdiocese, your Eminence, you must recognize nationwide implementation of such procedures would prevent the [name withheld] of the priesthood and the [name withheld] of the laity from further plundering their parishes' Sunday collections as they have so brazenly done for so many generations.

Finally, and while the prospect of virtually eliminating the incidence of Sunday collection theft is more than sufficient to justify decisive action at the national level, I would also call your attention to the fact that most church embezzlements are committed, in part, for the purpose of enabling the embezzler to finance some vice or perversion they might not otherwise pursue had the target of their embezzlement not been so vulnerable. [name withheld] vice, for example, was gambling, and [name withheld] perversion seems to have been the gay lifestyle coupled with extreme narcissism. We both know these men and their predilections are by no means isolated phenomena within our society or the Church. Absent effective concerted action at the USCCB level, I have no doubt their number will only increase.

As I stated in my correspondence with Archbishop Murphy in 1994, and repeated in correspondence with a number of your predecessors, I stand ready to assist in this formidable undertaking in any way you or the Conference may deem helpful. The Church's credibility and moral standing was critically injured as a result of the predator-priest scandal, and I sincerely believe the nationwide dissemination and implementation of genuinely secure Sunday collection guidelines would go a long way toward restoring the Church's once premier standing as the face and voice of Christendom.

I wish you a blessed Christmas and a fulfilling New Year in Christ's service,

Michael W. Ryan

January 3, 2008

OFFICE OF THE CARDINAL

Dear Mr. Ryan,

Thank you for your letter of December 17, which I've shared with the finance officer of the Archdiocese of Chicago, Mr. [name withheld]. He'll be writing you about the component of the financial guidelines that you mention in your letter to me.

Concerning the establishment of guidelines for all dioceses under the auspices of the USCCB, the advice you've been receiving from the Associate General Secretary has been accurate. The Church is not a corporation in this country, and the dioceses are administratively independent of the USCCB. Nevertheless, the ability to suggest guidelines and oversee financial practices began a few years ago when the suffragan dioceses in the metropolitan provinces agreed to give a report once a year on the functioning of their finance councils to the metropolitan archbishops. With this as a precedent, Mr. [name withheld], CPA, Chief Financial Officer of the Diocese of [name withheld], has brought together a committee that has begun to create guidelines for accounting practices and financial services in the dioceses in the United States. I believe the plan is to bring these forward and to submit them to the body of bishops as "best practices" for each diocese, with the understanding that dioceses will choose to implement them as they can. Except for those few instances in the code of canon law, particularly around liturgy and several financial issues relative to fundraising, the USCCB cannot legislate for particular dioceses, but it can "strongly encourage."

I would suggest you be in touch with Mr. [name withheld] and ask to be part of the conversation as it moves forward in shaping guidelines that will change our practices in this country in the years to come. Thank you very much for your concern for this issue, which is not only a matter of justice but also of the Church's being responsible to her faithful.

If you have any other further reflections, please let me know. In the meantime, you and your family are in my prayers; please keep me in yours.

Sincerely yours in Christ,

Francis Cardinal George, O.M.I.

Archbishop of Chicago

cc: Rev. [name withheld], General Secretary, USCCB

Mr. [name withheld], CPA, Chief Financial Officer, Diocese of [name withheld]

[letterhead]

December 1, 2010

PERSONAL & CONFIDENTIAL
Archbishop Timothy M. Dolan, President
U. S. Conference of Catholic Bishops
3211 Fourth Street, N.E.
Washington, DC 20017-1194

Dear Archbishop Dolan:

By way of introduction, I am a retired federal law enforcement official who, for the past 20 years, has lobbied the U.S. Conference of Catholic Bishops to promote the Church-wide adoption of genuinely secure Sunday collection procedures. I am writing to you in regard to that issue which I consider to be of vital importance to the future viability of the Church in America. I want to begin, however, by congratulating you on your recent election to succeed Cardinal George as President of the USCCB. This is a difficult time for our nation as well as for our Church, and I know you will seek the guidance of our Lord as you endeavor to lead your fellow prelates with wisdom and grace.

As I indicated, your Excellency, the purpose of this letter is to bring to your attention the great need for the Church-wide implementation of genuinely effective systems and procedures to protect the Church's principal source of revenue: the Sunday collection. The need I speak of does not merely concern fiscal accountability, although that is most definitely a principal aspect. But the moral aspect is of even greater importance. By failing to do what ought to be done, i.e., to implement genuinely secure collection procedures Church-wide, the hierarchy is tacitly approving an ongoing temptation to sin. In effect, the USCCB is seen to place the preservation of bishops' autonomy and temporal authority ahead of what is assumed to be a higher obligation to save souls, in this case, the souls of those who succumb to the great temptation to steal.

The fact that I am calling in 2010 for action that could and should have been initiated as much as 50 years earlier speaks volumes. Cases such as those involving Rev. [name withheld] at St. Martin of Tours Parish on Long Island, Rev. [name withheld] at St. John the Baptist Parish in Haverhill, MA, and Monsignor [name withheld] of "everyone-does-it" fame in Manhattan will continue to plague the Church in the years ahead unless and until the USCCB swallows its pride and does what it surely must know is the morally, fiscally and ethically right thing to do.

If I may be so bold as to offer a few suggestions, your Excellency, I would first urge you not to refer my letter to the USCCB staff for the preparation of yet another of the "we are not canonically empowered" replies I have received over the course of the past 20 years. I know the USCCB is not empowered, but I also know Canon 455 provides a means whereby it can become empowered. The reality, then, is that the Conference does not wish to be empowered because it does not wish to issue a general decree.

Based upon my past experience, I can also say your referral of my letter to the DFMC would be a fruitless gesture unless it was accompanied by a directive ordering them to prepare the Chicago guidelines for Church-wide dissemination. Clearly, the DFMC does what the USCCB asks them to do and skirts those areas they are told to avoid. Indeed, my past communications with them have typically been met with total silence. If you can believe it, even referrals by former NCCB/USCC Director of Finance Sister Frances Mlocek as well as your predecessor, Cardinal George, went unanswered.

I would also note that perceived differences between dioceses cannot be a basis for avoiding Church-wide implementation of secure procedures; that is because there is essentially only one protocol for effectively protecting the collections between basket and bank, and it does not vary based upon a parish's size or location. As information, your Excellency, I developed that protocol in the early 1990s and the Archdiocese of Chicago codified it in 2005 under its then Director of Finance [name withheld]. The protocol was subsequently disseminated archdiocese-wide as a "Best Practice" under the title *Management of Sunday Collections*. While it's not as detailed as my guidelines, it is far and away the best Church-issued guideline available.

Since then, the National Leadership Roundtable on Church Management has adopted the Chicago AD guidelines as one of their recommended Best Practices. Based upon a weakness that I detected in those guidelines, however, I authored an addendum which the NLRCM was kind enough to post for download with the Chicago guidelines at their website. While I doubt the guidelines have been fully implemented throughout the AD of Chicago, I do know they were instrumental in putting an end to at least one ongoing embezzlement involving Rev. [name withheld] at the parish of St. Margaret Mary.

Finally, your Excellency, I would be remiss if I failed to point out that collection thefts often involve, even abet, the pursuit of sinful activities. For example, Rev. [name withheld] and Rev. [name withheld] were involved with pornography while Rev. [name withheld], was involved in the gay life. One can only wonder whether these men would have gone astray in the ways they did if they had not had such easy access to highly vulnerable Sunday collections.

Each time we say the Confiteor, we acknowledge that we have sinned in what we have done and in what we have failed to do. Does the USCCB's refusal to implement truly secure collection procedures make its members ultimately responsible for the weekly collection thefts and the sins they represent? I believe most objective observers would say that it does.

I have published two articles on this subject, both available for download from my website, ChurchSecurity.info. Also available for download from my website are my Sunday collection guidelines as well as guidelines for protecting a parish's revenue after it has been deposited into the parish bank account. Everything is there for the taking, with no identity traps or other requirements.

I look forward to hearing from you, your Excellency, at such time as you have had an opportunity to consider the information contained herein and decide what action you will initiate as a result.

Sincerely,

Michael W. Ryan

Office of the President

3211 FOURTH STREET NE WASHINGTON DC 20017-1194
202-541-3100 FAX 202-541-3166
Most Reverend Timothy M. Dolan
Archbishop of New York

December 30, 2010

Dear Mr. Ryan,

Thank you for your letter of December 1, 2010 and for your kind words regarding my election as President of the USCCB.

Thank you also for your thoughts about the need for effective and transparent handling of the Sunday collection. As you note, this is a very important issue since it so personally connects the faithful with the work of their parishes and with the wider Church.

As your letter notes the USCCB is not authorized to issue a binding decree in this matter. However, I will gladly forward your letter and suggestion to Bishop Kevin Farrell of Dallas who is the Episcopal moderator of the Diocesan Fiscal Management Conference for his information and study.

Again, thank you, Mr. Ryan, for your concern for the appropriate care of Sunday donations.

Faithfully in Christ,

Most Reverend Timothy M. Dolan

Archbishop of New York

President, United States Conference of Catholic Bishops

cc: Bishop Kevin Farrell

[letterhead]

February 3, 2011

<u>PERSONAL AND CONFIDENTIAL</u>
Most Reverend Kevin J. Farrell, D.D.
Episcopal Moderator
Diocesan Fiscal Management Conference
Post Office Box 60210
San Angelo, TX 76906-0210

Dear Bishop Farrell:

I am writing to you in reference to Archbishop Dolan's letter of December 30, copy of which he referred to you together with my letter of December 1, 2010. As you know from that correspondence, I am concerned with the hierarchy's continuing failure to provide a uniformly effective level of protection for the Church's principal source of revenue, the Sunday collection. With the exception of its one-time Executive Director, Rev. [name withheld], all of my prior communications with the DFMC have been directed to its presidents and selected diocesan financial officers. I have corresponded extensively with various members of the USCCB (formerly the NCCB) and therefore saw no value in corresponding with your predecessor, Bishop Trautman. At Archbishop Dolan's implied suggestion, however, I am taking this opportunity to communicate with you.

As you know from my correspondence with Archbishop Dolan, I am absolutely satisfied that Canon 455 provides a means whereby the USCCB can become empowered to issue a general decree mandating how collections must be handled within the Conference's member dioceses and archdioceses. Indeed, the USCCB has issued a number of general decrees through the empowering provisions of Canon 455 since the current Code of Canon Law was promulgated in 1983. In light of that, the *we-are-not-empowered* declarations made by Archbishop Dolan and his predecessors, though technically true, seem less than candid if not downright misleading.

I have published two articles on this subject, Bishop Farrell, both of which can be downloaded from my website, ChurchSecurity.info. In addition, I'm presently working on a manuscript that is taking the shape of a detailed exploration of the sad state of affairs embodied by the USCCB's refusal to act. Practically speaking, there is only one method for effectively protecting a parish's collections, and I would like to be able to include the hierarchy's reason(s) for refusing to utilize Canon 455 and implement genuinely secure procedures nationwide. Thus far, however, I have been unable to elicit even one word from the USCCB regarding their nonfeasance in this vital area.

I look forward to hearing from you at your earliest opportunity.

Sincerely,

Michael W. Ryan

DIOCESE OF DALLAS

[Diocese's logo]

Office of the Bishop

February 14. 2011

Dear Mr. Ryan:

Thank you for the letter you sent regarding your previous correspondence of Archbishop Dolan, the United States Conference of Bishops, and the Diocesan Fiscal Management Conference.

Having worked for twenty years as the Chief Financial Officer of the Archdiocese of Washington, I read with interest your articles regarding "internal controls and the protection of collection funds." I regret to inform you that your interpretation of Canon 455 is incorrect. It is not within the authority of the Conference to mandate how collections should be handled. Every Bishop is responsible to assure that proper internal controls are in place in all institutions within his diocese.

I thank you for your concern and will bring it to the attention at the USCCB at my next meeting.

Faithfully in Christ,

Most Reverend Kevin J. Farrell, D.D.

Bishop of Dallas

(letterhead)

March 4, 2011

PERSONAL AND CONFIDENTIAL
Most Reverend Kevin J. Farrell, D.D.
Episcopal Moderator
Diocesan Fiscal Management Conference
Post Office Box 60210
San Angelo, TX 76906-0210

Dear Bishop Farrell:

Thank you for your letter of February 14 regarding my contention that the Code of Canon Law provides a means whereby the USCCB can become empowered to issue a general decree mandating how the collections must be handled Conference-wide. As noted in my letter of February 3, the means I'm referring to is Canon 455.

In your reply, you stated: "I regret to inform you that your interpretation of Canon 455 is incorrect. It is not within the authority of the Conference to mandate how collections should be handled." In saying my "interpretation of Canon 455 is incorrect," you seem to be implying that, even if it wished to do so, the USCCB is somehow prohibited from using the empowering provisions of Canon 455 to issue a general decree mandating how collections must be handled throughout the Conference's member dioceses and archdioceses.

If that inference is correct, Bishop Farrell, I would appreciate knowing what Church law or regulation bars the USCCB from using Canon 455 to issue a general decree involving the collections while, at the same time, allowing it to utilize Canon 455 to issue other decrees such as the Essential Norms created by the USCCB in 2002. To put it another way, the point I wish to clarify is not whether the USCCB presently possesses the authority to mandate how collections should be handled, but rather whether, with the approval of two thirds of the prelates who belong to the Conference and possess a deliberative vote, the USCCB can obtain that authority by employing the empowering provisions of Canon 455.

I apologize for what might seem to be excessive persistence, Bishop Farrell, but I do not want to ascribe a position to you or to the USCCB that is not completely accurate. I look forward to hearing from you at your earliest opportunity.

Sincerely,

Michael W. Ryan

[letterhead]

February 13, 1990

<u>PERSONAL ATTENTION</u>
Mr. [name withheld]
Administrator, National Office
Diocesan Fiscal Management Conference
680 W. Peachtree Street, NW
Atlanta, GA 30308-1964

Dear Mr. [name withheld]:

This refers to the January 24 letter of Sr. Frances Mlocek, Director of Finance, USCC, transmitting my proposal to establish an appropriate level of protection over the Sunday collection. I was pleased to note that Sr. Mlocek recognizes this area as being a matter of concern for many parishes.

There can be no doubt that the Church is losing large sums of money to surreptitious theft each and every week of the year. Our knowledge of human nature and the law of averages tells us that is the case. The only question is, "How much money is being lost?" A reasonable estimate cannot be formulated unless and until someone in authority recognizes and addresses the issue.

At the time I furnished my proposal to Sr. Mlocek, I failed to include a copy of the recommended transmittal form. A copy of that form is herewith. I envision it being a two-part form, the original of which would be attached to the sack hasp during the sealing process. I would be pleased to elaborate on the concept, if you wish to pursue it further.

Also enclosed is a copy of a letter that gives support to my cost estimates insofar as the sacks and seals are concerned. My estimate on the cost of transmittal forms was less directed, but I think you'll find it fairly realistic. There is one other item I didn't include, and that is a wire-cutter needed to remove the plastic seals; scissors won't do the job.

Finally, Mr. [name withheld], (just so you know where I'm coming from) when I first entered this area it was with a profit motive. Enclosed is a copy of my brochure which, together with a personal transmittal letter offering a <u>free</u> consultation, yielded not even one response from the nearly 100 pastors to whom it was directed. That dismal result convinced me that the issue can only be solved by action initiated at or above the archdiocesan level.

If you feel I can be of further assistance in any effort to resolve this critical issue, don't hesitate to contact me.

Sincerely,

Michael W. Ryan

[letterhead]

April 17, 1990

<u>PERSONAL ATTENTION</u>
Mr. [name withheld], Administrator
Diocesan Fiscal Management Conference
680 W. Peachtree Street, NW
Atlanta, GA 30308-1964

Dear Mr. [name withheld]:

This refers to my letter of February 13 concerning the collection security proposal referred to you by USCC Director of Finance Sr. Frances Mlocek. I assume you received my letter, and am writing at this time to furnish the particulars of a variation I developed for a particular parish.

A meeting with the pastor and members of his Finance Council resulted in two conclusions on their part. First, they agreed the existing procedures for handling the Sunday collection were seriously deficient and in need of immediate corrective action. Secondly, however, one or more of them felt the use of numbered seals and transmittal forms is unnecessary, and that an adequate level of security could be achieved without them.

While I felt and still feel those items offer the best means of ensuring a consistent level of security, I agreed to draw up alternative procedures based upon the group's wishes. A copy of the alternative procedures is herewith. I also prepared forms for documenting currency and coin counts, as well as a sample office layout detailing a recommended SOP for counting the collection. Copies of those exhibits are also herewith.

Finally, Mr. [name withheld], recognizing the sensitivity connected with the implementation of such changes, I prepared a letter that could be used by the pastor to notify his volunteer corps of the nature and rationale for the new procedures. A copy of that sample letter (the names are fictitious) is also herewith.

Working as I am in a strictly advisory capacity, it would be inappropriate for me to provide particulars regarding the results of the referenced installation. I respectfully suggest, however, that you consider launching two or more pilot installations for the purpose of assessing the effectiveness of these two systems, i.e., one utilizing numbered seals and transmittal forms, and the other only utilizing unnumbered seals. That approach will ensure a truly informed decision as to their actual and relative merits.

Again, if I may assist you in any way, don't hesitate to contact me.

Sincerely,

Michael W. Ryan

cc: w/enclosures Sr. Frances Mlocek, Director Of Finance, USCC

[letterhead]

April 17, 1990

PERSONAL ATTENTION
Sr. Frances Mlocek, IHM, CPA
Director of Finance
United States Catholic Conference
3211 4th Street N.E.
Washington, DC 20017-1194

Dear Sister Mlocek:

This refers to my letter of January 17 and your referral of
January 24 to [name withheld], Administrator, Diocesan Fiscal
Management Conference. Since then, I have corresponded with
[name withheld] on two occasions, the most recent being
concurrent with the date of this letter. Copies of my
correspondence and related exhibits are herewith as information.

The more I think about and observe (in an admittedly limited
way) the matter of collection security, Sister Mlocek, the more
convinced I become that the loss incidents which have
surfaced over the years are merely the tip of the iceberg. On a
national or diocesan level, the dollar loss figures have to be
staggering. If they haven't already done so, I'm sure your
expertise in the fields of accounting and human behavior will
eventually lead you to the same conclusion.

While I certainly can't describe myself as the voice of one
crying in the wilderness, I have begun to wonder whether the
Church will ever muster the intestinal fortitude needed to
confront and resolve the problems and issues surrounding this
highly critical subject. Unfortunately, each passing Sunday
represents lost revenue that can never be recaptured; with the
financial woes so prevalent within the Church today, that is a
truly sad state of affairs. We close churches, and worse yet -
schools, for mainly financial reasons, but no one seems willing
to lift a finger to curtail the cash losses everyone knows or
should know are occurring each and every Sunday of the year.

Somehow, Sr. Mlocek, I don't think you're the one who
needs to be harangued, and I apologize for doing so. If there's

anyone else to whom my concerns should be directed, please let me know; I consider the issue far too important to "throw in the towel" before exhausting every possible avenue of Church authority.

Sincerely,

Michael W. Ryan

enclosures

[letterhead]

January 11, 1994

<u>PERSONAL ATTENTION</u>
Rev. [name withheld], Ed.D.
Executive Director, DFMC
3225 Pickle Road
Oregon, OH 43616

Dear Father [name withheld]:

I am writing to you at the suggestion of Sister Frances Mlocek who recently forwarded to you a correspondence file concerning my several-year effort to create an adequate level of security over the Church's Sunday collection system. I assume Sister Mlocek included my handbook, Protecting the Purse, with her referral.

Since you and I don't know each other, I feel it is appropriate for me to briefly explain my motivation. I'm a retired federal law enforcement official with significant experience in the areas of financial accountability and internal security. I began to ponder the Church's lack of secure Sunday collection procedures in 1986, shortly before retiring. In early 1987, I began what proved to be a fruitless effort to stimulate interest at the local parish and diocesan levels. I offered a no-obligation, individual consultation with approximately 90 pastors; not one responded! I then directed my attention to the chancellor's office where I was eventually given a polite but unproductive audience. My subsequent NCCB contacts are well documented.

It was only after realizing the hierarchy wanted no part of a secure Sunday collection system that I developed my handbook. It's development was not motivated by profit; my retirement income is quite adequate. I wrote it because I thought (naively) individual pastors would recognize the value of a truly secure Sunday collection system. I advertised the handbook in the Archdiocese of Chicago weekly at a nominal price of $15 but sold only one copy; the pastor of my mother's parish bought it, but only after she brought the advertisement to his attention.

In follow-up correspondence, however, the pastor informed me that he felt his Sunday collection was already being handled securely and my system would therefore not be needed. I had occasion to observe how the Sunday collection was handled in his parish, and my mother had been involved in the counting process; his Sunday collection was <u>highly</u> vulnerable! I concluded, Father [name withheld], the pastor was actually motivated by the fact that my system excludes everyone (<u>including him</u>) from having lone, unobserved access to Sunday collection funds (or any portion thereof) prior to their deposit in the parish bank account. That's a harsh opinion, I know, but if you were on the receiving end of several years of dissembling and obfuscation, I dare say you might well come to the same conclusion.

Lest you conclude my system is untried, however, I'm pleased to report that it was implemented in at least one parish of which I am aware. As you might have guessed, I'm referring to my own parish which experienced a remarkable turnaround in <u>cash</u> receipts beginning with the very first Sunday. It's resulted in a revenue recovery of about $25,000 <u>per year</u>, but apparently that's of no interest to the hierarchy; I mentioned the phenomenon in letters to the cardinal and chancellor, but there was no follow-up. As a matter of fact, their written responses made no mention of what, in the corporate world, would have set off bells and whistles at all levels of the organization! It makes one wonder, doesn't it?

Well, now that you know where I'm coming from, Father [name withheld], I'll get to the second reason for this letter. Sister Mlocek indicated the Diocesan Fiscal Management Conference meets each year to discuss financial issues, and she suggested I consider offering to make a presentation. I would be willing to make a presentation, provided I was afforded sufficient notice and was treated like other guest speakers from the standpoint of expenses and speaking fees. I have no interest in being an exhibitor, because monetary profit is not my primary motivation. That said, however, I'd be remiss if I failed to mention that my handbook is protected by U. S. copyright laws and may not be used, copied or reproduced in any manner whatsoever without written permission.

If you do decide to explore the possibility of having me address your conference, you should understand that my presentation would make it abundantly clear the only acceptable collection security system is one that eliminates everyone (including the pastor) from having lone, unobserved access to the Sunday collection or any portion thereof, from the moment it is consolidated at the rear of the church until all funds have been counted and properly deposited in the parish bank account. Any system that fails to establish that level of security is merely window dressing!

I sent Sister Mlocek a personal note in December and included a syllogism I had constructed. She probably didn't include it in her referral, so I'm taking the liberty of including a copy for your information. At the risk of sounding "holier than thou" (I'm anything but), I close with a related (annotated) passage.

> Jesus said to his disciples, "Things that make people fall into sin are bound to happen, but how terrible for the one who makes [or knowingly allows?] them happen!"
>
> LUKE 17:1

Most sincerely,

Michael W. Ryan

[letterhead]

February 1, 2008

<u>PERSONAL ATTENTION</u>
Mr. [name withheld], CFO
Diocese of [name withheld]
[address]
[city, state & Zip]

Dear Mr. [name withheld]:

I am writing to you at the suggestion of USCCB President
Francis Cardinal George who copied you with his letter of
January 3 in reply to my letter of December 17 regarding the
need for Church-wide procedures for effectively securing the
Church's principal source of revenue: the Sunday collection.

According to Cardinal George, you are heading a committee
formed for the purpose of developing guidelines for accounting
practices and financial services throughout the Church in
America. As one who has been studying and promoting Sunday
collection security for the past 20 years, I believe I've developed
a unique insight insofar as the establishment of effective
Sunday collection procedures is concerned. In light of that, and
pursuant to Cardinal George's suggestion that I ask to be part
of the conversation as it moves forward in shaping new
national guidelines, please consider this letter to be both my
formal request to participate and my first contribution to the
conversation.

Given the unique nature of the Sunday collection, not the least
of which is the fact that it takes place in conjunction with a
solemn religious service, the use of commercial methods such
as cash registers and printed receipts are obviously not
feasible. The question then becomes how to best emulate
secure commercial methods without infringing upon or tainting
the spiritual solemnity of the environment in which the
collection is performed. Assuming the objective is to establish a
genuinely secure Sunday collection, there is really only one
basic protocol that will enable the accomplishment of that
objective.

No Sunday collection system can be truly secure, unless and until certain equipment and procedures have been applied to effectively preclude anyone from having lone, unobserved access to those funds. This mantle of protection must begin immediately after the collection is taken up - when the ushers meet to consolidate the collection into a single container - and must remain absolutely unbroken until all monies have been accurately tallied and properly deposited in the parish bank account.

In order to reach that objective, the container into which the funds collected for each Mass or service are consolidated must be of a type that can be closed and positively sealed. The act of sealing must be done immediately after the consolidation. On two-collection Sundays, the sealing of the 1st collection may not be delayed pending completion of the 2nd collection. Further, either the device used to secure the container or the container itself must be serially numbered and must be of a type that cannot be opened and reclosed without reflecting that act. This is necessary so that, from church vestibule to counting room, each person in the chain of custody will, through simple visual examination, be able to determine whether anyone had or could have had access to the funds contained therein.

Detailed written operating procedures must be developed for the collection, consolidation, transport, interim storage, counting and banking operations. The counting procedures must provide for the presence of at least three (3) counters (two are insufficient) before any sealed containers are opened, and establish continuous observation and control over the funds (especially the currency) by at least two (2) persons, from the moment the storage containers are unsealed and opened until the funds have been counted separately by two persons, verified, recorded on a witnessed bank deposit slip, and locked or sealed in a bank deposit bag. The use of rotating teams of counters is highly recommended.

Each week's count must be documented via standardized forms. These forms must be designed so that, when completed, they clearly reflect the serial numbers of the seals or sacks assigned for use by the ushers, the serial numbers of the seals or sacks received and processed by the counters, and whether the required witnessing and count verification procedures were followed. The forms must be reviewed and filed each week by someone not otherwise involved in the counting and banking process.

The above is only a brief outline of the minimum requirements, Mr. [name withheld]; complete guidelines go into greater detail to preclude any misunderstanding as to what is required to establish and maintain a genuinely secure Sunday collection system. If you would like to obtain a set of detailed guidelines in use at this writing, I recommend you visit the Chicago AD web site and download their procedures; their guidelines are contained in a document entitled *Management of Sunday Collections*, and are the most comprehensive I've seen. This is in contrast to the guidelines available at your website which, with all due respect, are clearly flawed and insufficient to deter or detect surreptitious theft. In that regard, the only condition worse than having no security whatsoever is having only an appearance or facade of security behind which any thief would be free to carry on their depredations.

Finally, Mr. [name withheld], I want to reiterate my great and abiding desire to help the Catholic Church in America accomplish a vital objective that, in all candor, could and should have been accomplished decades ago: the establishment of a genuinely effective level of security for the Church's principal source of revenue. I look forward to hearing from you at such time as you have had an opportunity to consider how my knowledge and experience might best be employed in that aspect of your committee's overall mission to develop guidelines for accounting practices and financial services that will effectively serve the needs of the Church in America in the years ahead.

Sincerely,

Michael W. Ryan

www.ChurchSecurity.info

[letterhead]

July 21, 2008

<u>PERSONAL ATTENTION</u>
Francis Cardinal George, President
U. S. Conference of Catholic Bishops
3211 Fourth Street, N.E.
Washington, D.C. 20017

Dear Cardinal George:

On December 17, 2007, I wrote you concerning the extreme vulnerability of Sunday collection funds in most dioceses throughout the United States. At that time, I also called your attention to the fact that most church embezzlements are committed, at least in part, for the purpose of enabling the embezzler to afford some vice or perversion they might not otherwise have pursued if the Sunday collection system had been effectively secured.

The nexus between vulnerable Sunday collection funds and the ability of wayward priests (and lay-persons) to fund their aberrant behaviors has thus far been largely ignored by the mainstream media in their coverage of the predator-priest scandal, and I look forward to the day when the media realizes the USCCB has steadfastly refused to effectively address this glaring deficiency in spite of overwhelming evidence that it has been <u>and remains</u> a key factor in the scandal. It's a classic case of nonfeasance.

In your January 3 reply, you referred me to [name withheld], CFO of the Diocese of [name withheld] and a member of the DFMC who was (and I presume still is) heading a committee that, in your words, *"has begun to create guidelines for accounting practices and financial services in the dioceses in the United States."* As you know from my letter of January 25, I expressed my intention to communicate with [name withheld], and I subsequently did so. As of this date, however, I have yet to receive the courtesy of an acknowledgement let alone a reply.

By his own count, as described in the 2008 Winter edition of the *Herald*, Mr. [name withheld's] Accounting Practices Committee is comprised of fifteen (15) CPAs, not counting three additional CPA advisors from public accounting firms. With that many CPAs reviewing the Church's accounting systems, one would think they would very quickly zero in on the absolute need to ensure that every dollar that is placed in the collection basket each weekend does, in fact, reach the bank. Instead, however, they focus on minutiae such as Canons 1262 and 1297 regarding fund-raising appeals and the leasing of church property. In comparison to the task of ensuring the safety of <u>the Church's principal source of revenue</u>, their focus can be likened to rearranging the deck chairs on the Titanic as it was sinking.

Bottom line, Cardinal George, the Church remains in a downward spiral due, in large measure, to the hierarchy's shocking refusal to <u>effectively</u> address difficult issues such as Sunday collection security.

Most sincerely,

Michael W. Ryan

www.ChurchSecurity.info

[letterhead]

August 15, 2008

PERSONAL ATTENTION
[name withheld], President
Diocesan Fiscal Management Conference
Post Office Box 60210
San Angelo, TX 76906

Dear Mr. [name withheld]:

I am writing this letter to make you aware of a particular issue concerning the Church's principal source of revenue, and to ask whether you can explain why action that could and should have been taken 50 years ago has yet to be taken. To be more specific, I would like to know why neither the USCCB nor the DFMC have moved to develop and implement uniformly secure procedures for protecting Sunday collection funds nationwide.

The answer most often given by the USCCB is that security of the collections is the exclusive domain of each local bishop, and the USCCB is not empowered to mandate how they will be handled. In saying that, however, they ignore the fact that Canon Law provides a basis for them to obtain authorization to issue guidelines that would apply conference-wide. What they are really saying, therefore, is that they do not wish to uniformly secure the Sunday collections. Anyone who maintains that security over the Church's principal source of revenue is best left to the discretion of local bishops and their staffs must, to be consistent, also maintain that the corporate offices of retailers such as Wal-Mart, Home Depot, Sears and Circuit City have no business mandating the manner in which individual outlets account for their sales revenue. We both know such a laissez faire policy would constitute sheer folly and, in addition to jeopardizing their very existence, would open the corporate officers to charges of nonfeasance or worse.

Late in 2007, I wrote Cardinal George (in his capacity as President of the USCCB) to express my ongoing concern for this glaring failure to act, and I asked that he make it a priority of his term of office. In his reply, he suggested I correspond with [name withheld] who he said was heading a committee "to create guidelines for accounting practices and financial services in the dioceses in the United States." I subsequently wrote to Mr. [name withheld] but failed to receive even the courtesy of an acknowledgement let alone a reply. I assume he hadn't had an opportunity to read or fully absorb the DFMC *Standards for Ethical Behavior & Professional Conduct.*

In any event, Mr. [name withheld], I can imagine no higher calling for the DFMC than to ensure the existence and application of a uniform, <u>genuinely effective</u> level of security over the Church's principal source of revenue, the Sunday collection. That obligation seems to have been recognized by the authors of the above referenced Standards in several statements, the most broadly worded of which declares: "We will implement policies and procedures to protect the resources of the Church from fraud, misuse and waste, and to provide accurate and reliable financial reporting."

I am well aware of the pecking order within the Church, and I know that you have no authority to dictate to the USCCB what they must do. Still, the DFMC is not without any means of persuasion, and I believe a righteous approach by the DFMC Board of Directors, perhaps a type of *white paper*, would provide the USCCB leadership with an incentive to stop dissembling and do the right thing. In that regard, I have written every USCCB (NCCB/USCC) President since Bishop Pilarczyk but have been singularly unsuccessful in my efforts to cause them to act in this vital matter. It seems they know they would have some very angry pastors on their hands and are fearful of being in any shorter supply of clergy than they already are. That, of course, is no excuse for their nonfeasance.

My efforts to enlist the interest of the DFMC date as far back as 1994 when Rev. [name withheld] was the Executive Director and, I now realize, the *gatekeeper* beyond whom nothing of a *controversial* nature passed. Like Mr. [name withheld], Rev. [name withheld] did not deem my letters worthy of acknowledgement. In his case, however, it appears he was occupied with what, to him, were more important matters. I trust you are not answerable to Rev. Trautman, the Episcopal Moderator. If that were the case, I would have no hope for DFMC action in this matter.

To my knowledge, the Archdiocese of Chicago is the only diocese in the country that has had the courage to implement genuinely effective Sunday collection procedures. Unfortunately, [name withheld], who I believe was the motivating force behind their implementation, has since left the Archdiocese, and I fear the guidelines might end up (if they haven't already) being widely ignored due to the absence of effective, ongoing follow-up. Those guidelines, incidentally, were closely modeled after guidelines that have been available for the taking at my website for the past 10+ years.

Finally, Mr. [name withheld], I hope you will take time to absorb the full import of the contents of this letter. There is a great deal more I could say in the matter, but I would suggest you visit my website and examine the documentation, articles and case histories I have made available there. The Church's continuing failure to implement in the 21st Century what should have been implemented in the 1950s or '60s is unconscionable and, in my opinion, renders the hierarchy ultimately responsible for every embezzlement committed as a result of their nonfeasance. Carry that one step further to the sins those embezzlements represent, as well as sins subsequently committed with the aid of those monies, and you can readily see the bishops have cause to be concerned for the safety of their souls. As Jesus himself phrased it, "Woe to the world because of things that cause sin! Such things must come, but woe to the one through whom they come!" [Matthew 18:7]

I look forward to hearing from you at such time as you have had an opportunity to review this matter and decide upon a course of action. If additional information is needed, please advise.

Most sincerely,

Michael W. Ryan

www.ChurchSecurity.info

----- Original Message -----

From: M. W. Ryan

To: Selected Recipients [fourteen members of the DFMC Board]

Sent: Sunday, February 22, 2009 4:19 PM

Subject: A Lenten request

Greetings;

I'm writing in follow-up to my email of November 24 which, for the record, was directed to thirteen (13) DFMC Officers and members, not one of whom acknowledged its receipt. Under normal circumstances, that would appear to be a shocking result, but my past experience with the Conference (which dates back to 1990) renders the result more or less standard operating procedure for DFMC communications.

In fairness, however, I note that my prior email (appended below) did not include a specific request for acknowledgment, and that might possibly account for the result. Still, prior written correspondence to Accounting Practices Committee Chairman [name withheld] and, subsequently, then President [name withheld] also went unacknowledged in spite of my clearly expressed desire to hear back from each of those gentlemen.

What I find especially noteworthy about [name withheld's] failure to reply is the fact that I was referred to him by USCCB President Cardinal George, a fact I mentioned in my letter to [name withheld]. Were I [name withheld], nothing short of a permission slip from Cardinal George (or Bishop Trautman) would have kept me from replying. Even then, however, my Christian upbringing and professional career would not have allowed me to ignore such correspondence. Every written inquiry deserves a written response; it's common courtesy.

In any event, I find the DFMC's unwillingness to discuss (let alone address) the extreme vulnerability of the Church's principal source of revenue both stunning and appalling. Because of that, I will share with you what I view as the most likely excuses for the failure of the DFMC to act upon this nationwide deficiency which so clearly begs to be addressed.

Excuse #1: The DFMC has been informed that the USCCB is not empowered to direct how Sunday collections will be handled in the various dioceses and archdioceses, that authority being the exclusive purview of the local bishops. Consequently, the DFMC's development of a standardized procedure would be pointless.

Response: The USCCB's claim of inability to act is a *red herring.* Canon 455 clearly provides the means by which conferences may request authority to issue "general decrees" for conference-wide application. While they will never admit it and, consequently, for reasons best known to its past and present leaders, the USCCB does not wish to issue guidelines they know would bring a virtual end to the phenomenon of Sunday collection embezzlement.

Excuse #2: Differences between dioceses and parishes preclude one set of guidelines being suitable for all. For this reason, the matter is best addressed by each diocese developing its own unique standards.

Response: While the Sunday collection may be unique to the Roman Catholic Church, it is essentially the same from parish to parish, varying only by dollar amount and number of individuals involved in its collection, transport, storage, counting and banking, the very operations for which minimum standards can and must be established to ensure that every dollar placed in the collection baskets on Saturday evening or Sunday morning does, if fact, reach the bank. Anyone who claims there is more than one practical way to effectively secure the Sunday collection either doesn't know what they're talking about or has ulterior motives for taking that position.

Excuse #3: The DFMC is precluded from acting in the matter, either because of limitations built into its charter or a (most likely unwritten) USCCB directive prohibiting DFMC involvement.

Response: In paragraph 21 of your *Standards for Ethical Behavior & Professional Conduct,* you state "*We will implement policies and procedures to protect the resources of the Church from fraud, misuse and waste, and to provide accurate and reliable financial reporting.*" That strikes me as a pretty clear commitment to revenue protection, and what better starting point could there be than the point where the majority of the Church's monetary resources is initially received. I leave it to you to answer the question of whether the USCCB has prohibited you from acting in the matter. Frankly, I wouldn't be at all surprised.

Excuse #4: Most if not all diocesan fiscal managers oversee parish-level audit programs and would take appropriate action to secure any parish's Sunday collection a diocesan audit showed to be in jeopardy.

Response: With all due respect, you can't audit what isn't there and, by their very nature, virtually all Sunday collection embezzlements are committed before the funds have been counted and recorded. The AICPA said it best when they declared "..... *agreement of a cash count with the recorded balance does not provide evidence that all cash received has been properly recorded. This illustrates an unavoidable distinction between fiduciary and recorded accountability: the former arises immediately upon acquisition of an asset; the latter arises only when the initial record of the transaction is prepared.*" In the case of a Sunday collection, fiduciary accountability begins when members of the congregation place their offerings in the collection basket. In a typical parish, however, several people (clergy, employees and volunteers) have lone, unobserved access to the collection or a portion thereof prior to its tabulation and deposit.

You might well be able to articulate one or more additional excuses for the DFMC's failure to effectively protect the Church's principal source of revenue. But no matter how many excuses you come up with, they're only excuses; there neither is nor ever can be a valid reason for the DFMC's failure to act in this matter.

When I ponder the hierarchy's knowing inaction in light of the great temptation to sin highly vulnerable Sunday collections constitute, I am invariably reminded of two things. The first is Jesus' admonition to his disciples: "*Things that cause sin will inevitably occur, but woe to the person through whom they occur.*" [Luke 17:1] The second thing that comes to my mind is *nonfeasance*: failure to do what ought to be done. And I ask myself how, Sunday after Sunday, bishops can stand on the altar, and DFMC officials can stand in the pews, reciting the *Confiteor* and not feel a twinge of conscience when uttering the words "*and in what I have failed to do*".

Frankly, it would tear me up to know I had allowed myself to be cowed into silence or inaction on a clear-cut matter of faith and morals. The extensive and painfully detailed coverage of the predator-priest scandal strongly suggests that a number of bishops have become immune to feelings of guilt and personal responsibility. It's time for the laity, especially those in positions of authority, to force this issue and bring to fruition what could and should have been accomplished two generations ago.

May this Lenten period be a time of deep introspection and spiritual renewal for us all,

M. W. Ryan

www.ChurchSecurity.info

Diocese of [name withheld]

February 23, 2009

Dear Mr. Ryan:

This letter is in response to your letter of February 1, 2008. Please accept my sincere apology for not responding sooner. I was recently reminded of your letter as a result of an email you sent to [name withheld], which he forwarded to me.

I am currently the chairman of the Accounting Practices Committee (APC) whose primary purpose is to represent the U.S. Catholic Church before regulatory bodies in the formulation of accounting principles and reporting standards that affect the Catholic Church. Typically these bodies are the Financial Accounting Standards Board and the American Institute of Certified Public Accountants.

The APC has created *Diocesan Financial Issues*, which is published by the USCCB and provides guidance on accounting and financial issues that are unique to Catholic Dioceses. The manual contains a chapter on financial governance. The chapter contains general guidance in the area of financial governance, including sample policies related to financial governance, but does not address specific procedures.

Thank you very much for your thoughts with regard to securing parish offertory. I will retain your letter for future reference and consider it a resource for developing sound parish offertory procedures.

Thank you, also, for your commitment to the Catholic Church and your offer to assist the Church in this matter.

Sincerely yours,

[name withheld], CPA

Chief Financial Officer

[letterhead]

March 3, 2009

<u>PERSONAL ATTENTION</u>
Mr. [name withheld], Chairman
Accounting Practices Committee
Diocesan Fiscal Management Conference
Post Office Box 60210
San Angelo, TX 76906

Dear Mr. [name withheld]:

Thank you for your letter of February 23 concerning my letter of February 1, 2008 that was directed to you at the suggestion of USCCB President Francis Cardinal George.

If I understand your reply correctly (and reading between the lines), neither you nor the Accounting Practices Committee you chair have been tasked with the responsibility of developing comprehensive procedures for securing the Church's principal source of revenue: the Sunday collection. As I read it, your mission and that of your Committee is to "represent" the Church before regulatory bodies such as the Financial Accounting Standards Board and the American Institute of Certified Public Accountants (AICPA) of which you are a member.

Again reading between the lines, I gather your primary focus and that of your Committee is <u>not</u> upon accounting and financial issues relating to parish operations where the bulk of the Church's revenue (much of it in the form of loose cash) is first received, but rather upon diocesan operations where most if not all of the revenue received is in the form of secure, non-negotiable instruments. Assuming my understanding is correct (your publication *Diocesan Internal Controls* seems to support that), I can only shake my head in astonishment at the almost total lack of concern the Church's fiscal experts (arguably its fiscal *watchdog*) have for the Church's principal source of revenue.

You mentioned representing the American Catholic Church before the AICPA, Mr. [name withheld], and I wonder how you or any member of the DFMC could be comfortable doing so, knowing the Church's principal source of revenue has been afforded <u>none</u> of the protections called for by the AICPA's own standards as contained in their 1972 authoritative guideline entitled *Statement on Auditing Standards - Codification of Auditing Standards and Procedures.* Sections 320.42, .44 and .67 of those guidelines, for example, are highly relevant to a financial operation such as the Sunday collection.

While the Church could and should have applied readily available security procedures and equipment as long ago as the 1950s, the AICPA's 1972 guidelines surely constituted the basis for prompt creation of effective measures establishing a uniform level of protection for the Sunday collection <u>nationwide</u>. Yet here we are nearly 40 years later with the Sunday collection in virtually every diocese in the nation as vulnerable to surreptitious theft in 2009 as it was in 1909!

You and I know what's going on, Mr. [name withheld]; the bishops want nothing to do with a genuinely secure Sunday collection system. Since they refuse to admit it, however, we're left to speculate on our own as to their motives. One only need review (as I have) the embezzlement case histories that have been aired in the media over the course of the past 20 years to recognize one very plausible motive: a large percentage of the embezzlers (by my count, over 50%) are members of the clergy, and we both know the lengths to which a disturbing number of bishops went to protect sexual-predator priests. Couple that with the fact that an unknown but no doubt significant number of those predator priests financed their heinous predations by pilfering unprotected Sunday collection funds, and I believe we're seeing the very face of evil. Indeed, I can't imagine what could be more evil than the purported guardians of morality financing the commission of sexual crimes through their <u>knowing and intentional</u> nonfeasance.

At this point, you're probably saying to yourself *"Why is this man telling me all this? I'm just a small cog in a big wheel; I don't call the shots!"* I'll go one step further, Mr. [name withheld], and allow that you might well even have been told Sunday collection security is not a matter for you, your Committee or the DFMC itself to worry about; that it is, in fact, forbidden territory. No matter what justification you may offer as the basis for the DFMC's inaction, it neither is nor ever can be valid. I realize we're in the midst of a great economic upheaval, making positions at your level something to be prized and protected. But some injustices and iniquities are of such great import they demand remedial action by those in a position to act in some way, even if such persons lack the power to completely remedy the situation. I have no doubt the hierarchy's de facto conspiracy of nonfeasance meets that definition.

In my August 15, 2008 letter to then DFMC President [name withheld], I acknowledged that he has no authority to dictate to the USCCB what they must do. I also noted, however, the DFMC is not without any means of persuasion, and I suggested the Board of Directors issue a *white paper* that could well provide the USCCB leadership with an incentive to stop dissembling and do the right thing. I now make that same suggestion to you, Mr. [name withheld]. The alternative, as I see it, is for you and the DFMC Board of Directors to wait for this scandalous situation to be aired in the mainstream media. When that day comes, the USCCB's "We are not empowered" mantra will be seen for what it is: a shameful and thoroughly discredited *red herring* unworthy of moral men, let alone prominent religious leaders. Then, the primary questions for the DFMC will revolve around what efforts, if any, it made to show the bishops the error of their position. How would you and [name withheld] answer that question today?

Most sincerely,

Michael W. Ryan

cc: [name withheld], President
     Diocesan Fiscal Management Conference

     Francis Cardinal George, President
     U. S. Conference of Catholic Bishops

Endnotes

[1] James D. Ratley, "2006 Report to the Nation on Occupational Fraud & Abuse," Association of Certified Fraud Examiners, Inc., 2006, 2

[2] "2006 Report to the Nation on Occupational Fraud & Abuse," Association of Certified Fraud Examiners, 2006, 6

[3] "2008 Report to the Nation on Occupational Fraud & Abuse," Association of Certified Fraud Examiners, 2008, 5

[4] Ibid., 4, 5, 8 and 12

[5] Richard Higgins, "Arrest of Lay Leader Stuns Catholic Parish in Conn.," *Boston Globe*, 25 March 1983

[6] Ibid.

[7] "Theft of Donations Draws 8-Year Term," Associated Press, 31 January 1993

[8] "Priest indicted in theft of funds from parish," *Providence Journal* (Providence, RI), 9 November 1990, A-1

[9] Center for Applied Research in the Apostolate, "Frequently Requested Church Statistics," 2011, http://cara.georgetown.edu/CARAServices/requestedchurchstats.html

[10] Roger Conner, "Catholic Charities USA Releases Data on National Disaster Services," Catholic Charities USA, 3 December 2010, http://www.catholiccharitiesusa.org/NetCommunity/Page.aspx?pid=2272

[11] U.S. Conference of Catholic Bishops, "The Catholic Church in America – Meeting Real Needs in Your Neighborhood," August 2006, http://www.usccb.org/comm/cip.shtml#toc24

[12] P. J. Kenedy, "Official Catholic Directory Anno Domini 2002," (New Providence, N.J.: P.J. Kenedy & Sons, 2002)

[13] "2008 Report to the Nation on Occupational Fraud & Abuse," Association of Certified Fraud Examiners, 2008, 4

[14] "2002 Report to the Nation, Occupational Fraud and Abuse," Association of Certified Fraud Examiners, 2002, 4

[15] Michelle Nicolosi, "With abuse came theft from church," *Seattle Post-Intelligencer*, 29 October 2004, www.seattlepi.com/local/article/With-abuse-came-theft-from-church-1158086.php

[16] Steve Rubenstein, "S.F. archdiocese slapped with sex suit," *San Francisco Chronicle*, 12 February 2003

[17] Paul Tennant, "Ex-pastor accused of taking $83K from parish," *Eagle Tribune* (North Andover, MA), 7 November 2010

[18] Richard Wronski, "Parish business manager faces charge he stole over $600,000," *Chicago Tribune*, 15 December 2005

[19] Sam Lucero, "Church embezzlement is theft, but also betrayal of trust," *Catholic Herald* (Milwaukee, WI), 8 January 2004

[20] Ibid.

[21] Ibid.

[22] Laura Keys, "New light shed on Fr Skehan case," *Kilkenny People* (Kilkenny, Ireland), 14 May 2009 www.kilkennypeople.ie/news/local/new_light_shed_on_fr_skehan_case_1_21 66311

[23] Brian Haas, "Former Delray Beach priests who stole money both going to prison," *South Florida Sun-Sentinel*, 25 March 2009, www.sun-sentinel.com/news/palm-beach/delray-beach/sfl-flpskehan0325pnmar25,0,4336023.story

[24] Committee on Auditing Standards, American Institute of Certified Public Accountants, "Statement on Auditing Standards - Codification of Auditing Standards and Procedures," 1973, Section 320.44, Copyright 1973. American Institute of Certified Public Accountants. Inc. All rights reserved. Used with permission.

[25] Ibid., Section 320.42

[26] Merriam-Webster, "Merriam-Webster's Collegiate Dictionary" 2000

[27] Committee on Auditing Standards, American Institute of Certified Public Accountants, "Statement on Auditing Standards - Codification of Auditing Standards and Procedures," 1973, Section 320.67, Copyright 1973. American Institute of Certified Public Accountants. Inc. All rights reserved. Used with permission.

[28] Ibid., Section 110.02

[29] Marcia Froelke Coburn, "Betrayal," *Chicago Magazine*, December 2007

[30] Center for Applied Research in the Apostolate, "Frequently Requested Church Statistics," 2010 http://cara.georgetown.edu/CARAServices/requestedchurchstats.html

[31] Office of Media Relations, United States Conference of Catholic Bishops, "The Catholic Church in the United States At A Glance," 31 December 2009, www.usccb.org/comm/catholic-church-statistics.shtml

[32] Sam Lucero, "Church embezzlement is theft, but also betrayal of trust," *Catholic Herald* (Milwaukee, WI), 8 January 2004

[33] Ibid.

[34] Ibid.

[35] Office for Parish Finances, Archdiocese of Milwaukee, "Parish Financial Management Manual," March 2009 http://www.archmil.org/ArchMil/Resources/2009PFMM.pdf

[36] Ibid.

[37] The Canon Law Society Of Great Britain And Ireland, "The Code of Canon Law," 1983 http://www.jcu.edu/Bible/480/Codex/1983code.htm

[38] Canon Law Society of America, "Code of Canon Law," 1999 http://www.vatican.va/archive/ENG1104/_P4Q.HTM

[39] Canon Law Society of America, "Code of Canon Law," 1999 http://www.vatican.va/archive/ENG1104/_P1L.HTM

[40] United States Conference of Catholic Bishops, "Index of Complementary Norms," 2011, http://www.nccbuscc.org/norms

[41] Wilton D. Gregory, USCCB President, "We Have Been Enlightened," 2002, http://usccb.org/comm/enlightened.shtml

[42] Avery Cardinal Dulles, "True and False Reform," *First Things*, August/September 2003. http://www.firstthings.com/article/2008/08/true-and-false-reform-31

[43] Ibid.

[44] Committee on Budget and Finance, National Conference of Catholic Bishops, "Diocesan Internal Controls, A Framework," 1995 http://www.usccb.org/finance/internal.shtml

[45] U.S. Conference of Catholic Bishops, "Index of Complementary Norms," http://www.usccb.org/norms

[46] Merriam-Webster, "Merriam-Webster's Collegiate Dictionary," 2000

[47] Libreria Editrice Vaticana, "Catechism of the Catholic Church," 1993 http://www.vatican.va/archive/ENG0015/_P80.HTM

[48] U.S. Conference of Catholic Bishops, "Charter for the Protection of Children and Young People," 2002

[49] Letter from Governor Frank A. Keating to USCCB President Wilton D. Gregory, June 2003 http://www.nccbuscc.org/comm/archives/2003/03-128.shtml

[50] Philip Messing, Denise Buffa and Marsha Kranes, "Priest's Pillage $hocker," *New York Post*, 10 October 2003

[51] U.S. Conference of Catholic Bishops, "Index of Complementary Norms," http://www.usccb.org/norms

[52] Ibid.

[53] http://dfmconf.org/

[54] Diocesan Fiscal Management Conference, "DFMC Strategic Plan," 2003

[55] Strategic Planning Committee, Diocesan Fiscal Management Conference, "Standards for Ethical Behavior & Professional Conduct," 29 April 2005

[56] Canon Law Society of America, "Code of Canon Law," http://www.vatican.va/archive/ENG1104/__P4R.HTM 1999

[57] Office of Financial Services, Diocese of Erie, PA "Parish Financial Practices Policy Manual," July 2008 www.eriercd.org/financemanual.asp

[58] Strategic Planning Committee, "Standards for Ethical Behavior & Professional Conduct," Diocesan Fiscal Management Conference, 29 April 2005

[59] Automatic Car Seal Company, "Automatic Car Seal," *The Railway Age*, 3 January 1908, 133

[60] Claim Department, "To the Editors," *The Railway Age*, 3 January 1908, 71

[61] Committee on Auditing Standards, American Institute of Certified Public Accountants, "Statement on Auditing Standards - Codification of Auditing Standards and Procedures," 1973

[62] Canon Law Society of America, "Code of Canon Law," 1999 http://www.vatican.va/archive/ENG1104/__P1L.HTM

[63] Ibid.

[64] Thomas P. Doyle, "CURRICULUM VITAE," August 2007 http://www.attorneygeneral.jus.gov.on.ca/inquiries/cornwall/en/hearings/exhibits/Tom_Doyle/pdf/01_Doyle_CV.pdf

[65] F. Ray Mouton, J.D. and Rev. Thomas P. Doyle, O.P. J.C.D., "The Problem of Sexual Molestation by Roman Catholic Clergy : Meeting the Problem in a Comprehensive and Responsible Manner," 9 June 1985, http://www.bishop-accountability.org/reports/1985_06_09_Doyle_Manual/

[66] Louise I Gerdes, "Child Sexual Abuse in the Catholic Church," (San Diego: Greenhaven Press, 2003)

[67] Louise I. Gerdes. "Introduction." At Issue: Child Abuse in the Catholic Church. Ed. Louise I. Gerdes. San Diego: Greenhaven Press, 2003. August 2004. 21 February 2011. http://www.enotes.com/catholic-child-abuse-article/38969.

Church Revenue Protection
www.ChurchSecurity.info

Made in the USA
Lexington. KY
03 February 2013